Windows 10 for the Older Generation

Jim Gatenby

BERNARD BABANI (publishing) LTD
The Grampians
Shepherds Bush Road
London W6 7NF
England

www.babanibooks.com

Please Note

Although every care has been taken with the production of this book to ensure that all information is correct at the time of writing and that any projects, designs, modifications and/or programs, etc., contained herewith, operate in a correct and safe manner and also that any components specified are normally available in Great Britain, the Publishers and Author do not accept responsibility in any way for the failure (including fault in design) of any project, design, modification or program to work correctly or to cause damage to any equipment that it may be connected to or used in conjunction with, or in respect of any other damage or injury that may be so caused, nor do the Publishers accept responsibility in any way for the failure to obtain specified components.

Notice is also given that if equipment that is still under warranty is modified in any way or used or connected with home-built equipment then that warranty may be void.

© 2016 BERNARD BABANI (publishing) LTD

First Published – January 2016

British Library Cataloguing in Publication Data:

A catalogue record for this book is available from the British Library

ISBN 978-0-85934-758-7

Cover Design by Gregor Arthur

Printed and bound in Great Britain for Bernard Babani (publishing) Ltd

About this Book

Windows 10 is the latest version of the Microsoft Windows operating system, used on most of the world's desktop and laptop computers. An operating system manages all of the essential functions, including the user interface through which you control your device. So a good knowledge of the operating system is vital if you're to make the best use of any computer — desktop, laptop, tablet or smartphone.

Even if you're new to computing, the plain English and absence of technical jargon in this book should help you to gain confidence and quickly acquire the basic skills needed.

The development of Microsoft Windows leading up to Windows 10 is described, including its impressive new features making it compatible with all computers from desktops to tablets and smartphones. Both touchscreen and mouse and keyboard operation are also covered.

Setting up and personalising Windows 10 is explained, whether you're buying a new machine or upgrading an existing one. Also Ease of Access features which give help with special needs such as mobility, hearing and eyesight. The new Windows apps described include the Cortana voice controlled personal assistant and the Microsoft Edge Web browser. The Skype free service for worldwide video calls is discussed as well as the Photos app for importing and managing images. Saving and managing files such as documents and photos is covered, including the OneDrive "cloud" storage system on the Internet, where files are accessible from anywhere and on any type of computer.

This book is intended to help you get started with Windows 10, which is already one of the leading operating systems on computers, tablets and smartphones.

About the Author

Jim Gatenby trained as a Chartered Mechanical Engineer and initially worked at Rolls-Royce Ltd., using computers in the analysis of jet engine performance. He then obtained a Master of Philosophy degree in Mathematical Education and taught maths and computing for many years to students of all ages and abilities, in school and in adult education.

The author has written over forty books in the fields of educational computing and Microsoft Windows, including the best-selling "Computing for the Older Generation". His most recent books have included "An Introduction to the Nexus 7", "Android Tablets Explained For All Ages", "An Introduction to the hudl 2" and "An Introduction to Android 5 Lollipop", all of which have been very well received.

Trademarks

Microsoft Windows, OneDrive, Cortana, Edge, Bing, OneNote, Xbox, Skype and Office 365 are trademarks or registered trademarks of Microsoft Corporation. Dropbox is a trademark or registered trademark of Dropbox Inc. Google Drive is a trademark or registered trademark of Google Inc. All other brand and product names used in this book are recognized as trademarks or registered trademarks, of their respective companies.

Acknowledgements

I would like to thank my wife Jill and our son David for their help and support during the preparation of this book. Also Michael Babani for making the project possible.

Contents

3

4

5

6

9

10

11

The Evolution of Windows 10

Early Operating Systems

Text Based Operating Systems

The first desktop computers, initially known as *microcomputers*, were controlled by text-based operating systems. The user typed in commands in the form of words at a prompt on the screen. For example:

A> PRINT ←⏎

The command was carried out after the user pressed the Return or Enter key.

Two of the most successful early operating systems were *CP/M* (*Control Program for Microcomputers*) from Digital Research and *MS-DOS*, (*Microsoft Disk Operating System*), often referred to as *DOS*. These required users to learn a lengthy list of commands, just to operate a desktop computer and carry out basic tasks such as saving and printing documents, etc. Obviously this was a complex task and, in the early days, computing was the province of specialists rather than the general user, as it is today.

The Graphical User Interface (GUI)

To make computers easier for everyone to use, first Apple and then Microsoft developed *Graphical User Interfaces*. These allowed the user to operate the computer more easily by *pointing and clicking* objects on the screen with a *mouse* rather than learning a long list of commands.

Microsoft Windows 1.0 is Launched

In 1985 Microsoft Windows 1.0 was released, introducing a *Graphical User Interface* (*GUI*). This displayed programs in rectangular boxes, i.e. *windows*, on the screen. Shown below is a screenshot from an earlier version of Microsoft Windows displaying two windows on the screen, simultaneously running two different programs — Microsoft Publisher and Windows Paint.

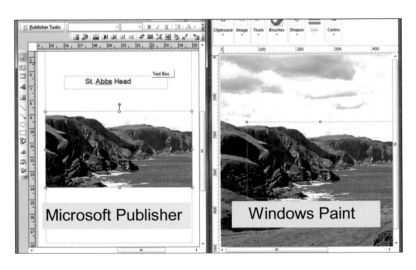

Menus and Icons

The Windows GUI also introduced *menus*, such as the **File** menu shown on the right, with lists of options which could be launched or executed by simply pointing and clicking with a *mouse*. There were also clickable *icons* or small images representing tasks such as to **Save** a file, such as a *photo*, as shown on the right.

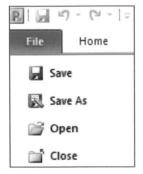

Versions of Microsoft Windows

There have been many versions of Microsoft Windows, often referred to as simply "Windows", but some of the editions most relevant to Windows 10 are listed below, together with the years when they were released.

Windows XP	2001
Windows 7	2009
Windows 8	2011
Windows 8.1	2013
Windows 10	2015

There were also different editions for home users, professional and small business users, education and large enterprises.

At the time of writing Microsoft Windows, in its various editions, is by far the most popular operating system on desktop and laptop computers. Windows XP still has many users while Windows 7 currently has the biggest worldwide share. Windows 8 and Windows 8.1 have recently seen a steady increase in their popularity.

Windows XP and Windows 7 were launched at times when desktop and laptop computers were prevalent. These devices are operated by a *mouse* or *touch pad* and a *physical keyboard*. Recent years have seen an explosion in the use of *touchscreen* tablets and smartphones and Windows 8 was developed in an attempt to satisfy the needs of users of both mice and keyboards as well as users of touchscreen devices.

Windows 7

Although this book is primarily about Windows 10, its design has been heavily influenced by the reaction of users to earlier versions such as Windows 7 and Windows 8/8.1.

The next few pages describe some of the features in Windows 7 and Windows 8/8.1 which contributed to the evolution of Windows 10.

The Windows 7 Start Menu

As shown below in Windows 7, the main way of launching programs was by the *Start Menu* on the left of the screen. The Start Menu in Windows 7 is very popular with users, giving easy access to favourite programs, as well as to major system features such as the **Control Panel**, which is still important in Windows 10.

The Windows 7 Start Menu

The Windows 7 Desktop

Apart from the popular Start Menu just described, the full-screen *Windows Desktop* makes it easy to tailor your computer to suit your own preferences and interests.

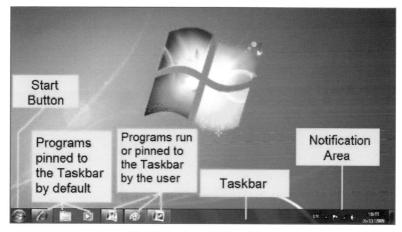

The Windows 7 Desktop

Shown above left is the *Start Button* used to launch the Start Menu shown on the previous page. The *Taskbar* along the bottom of the Desktop contains a number of icons to launch various programs. Several icons for important apps are pre-installed on the Taskbar, such as the *Windows Explorer*, now known as the *File Explorer*. You can also *pin* icons for your favourite programs onto the Taskbar. The Taskbar displays icons and also bigger *thumbnails* (small images) for programs currently running. On the right of the Taskbar is the *Notification Area* giving information such as the date, time and Internet connection status. You can change the background *wallpaper* on the Desktop and add icons to launch favourite programs, folders and websites.

Windows 8

Windows 8 was Microsoft's attempt to produce an operating system which would serve not only laptop and desktop computers but also the burgeoning number of touchscreen tablet computers and smartphones.

Microsoft designed Windows 8 with a radically new *tiled* Start Screen. The Start Screen appears as soon as the computer is fired up and it fills the whole of the screen.

The Windows 8 Start Screen

The tiles represent apps which can be launched by tapping with a finger or, on desktop and laptop computers, clicking with a mouse. There are tiles to launch your e-mail app and Internet Explorer, for example and "live" tiles showing the latest news and weather, continually updated. There is also a tile for the *Windows Store*, from which you can install additional apps or programs. You can pin tiles for your favourite apps or Web sites to the Start Screen and move, resize and delete tiles.

Windows 8 Surface Tablets

Microsoft also launched their own touchscreen *Surface* and *Surface Pro* tablets running *Windows RT* (a version of Windows 8) and *Windows 8 Pro* respectively. There is also a smartphone version known as Windows Phone 8.

Windows 8 on a Microsoft Surface Tablet

Windows 8.1

There was criticism of Windows 8 from users of desktop and laptop computers because the very popular Start Menu, shown on page 4, was no longer present. In addition, the familiar Windows Desktop, shown on page 5, although still accessible via a tile, does not appear on starting up.

Windows 8.1 introduced some changes to counteract some of these criticisms. These included a new Start button, but not a Start Menu as used in Windows 7. There was also an option to start up in the familiar Windows Desktop and a button to launch the All apps screen.

However, many users of mouse operated laptop and desktop computers saw no reason to upgrade to Windows 8.1. Consequently there were still many millions of users of Windows 7 and, to a lesser extent, Windows XP.

Windows 10

Windows 10 was released on the 29th July, 2015. Despite the criticism of Windows 8/8.1, many millions of copies of those operating systems were in use at the time. However, with even more users staying with Windows 7, it was clearly necessary for Microsoft to make Windows 10 more attractive to them. Microsoft introduced the *Windows Insider Program*, in which several million users worldwide are testing Windows 10 as it is developed and providing feedback to Microsoft as part of an ongoing program.

In order to encourage reluctant users, particularly of Windows 7, to upgrade to Windows 10, the new operating system is being offered as a free upgrade for a year, to existing users of Windows 7 and also Windows 8/8.1.

Reviews suggest that Microsoft have produced a very good operating system suitable for a range of devices — desktop, laptop, 2-in-1, tablet and smartphone, etc. Early reports stated that Windows 10 already had over 110 million users. A screenshot from Windows 10 is shown below.

The Windows 10 Start Menu

Most significantly, Windows 10 brings back a *Start Menu* launched by the *Start* button at the bottom left of the screen. The computer also starts up displaying the familiar Windows Desktop with the Taskbar along the bottom.

So the users of computers with mice and keyboards now have, in Windows 10, the Windows 7 features which were missing in Windows 8/8.1.

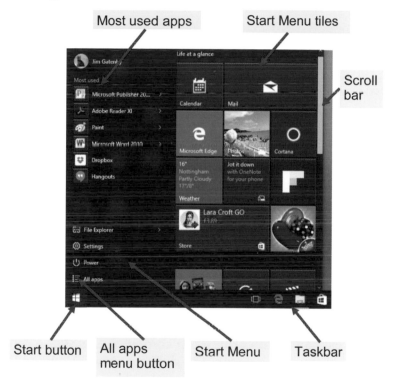

Unlike Windows 7, the tiled Start Menu area above can be scrolled or re-sized by dragging and dropping. New tiles can be pinned to the Start Menu, moved, resized or deleted. If preferred, all of the tiles can be deleted.

As shown on page 9, major changes in Windows 10 were the return of the Start Menu, similar to the Start Menu in Windows 7. Also the shrinking of the full-screen tiled Start Screen to one whose size can be controlled by the user or removed altogether if required. Another major change was the removal of the *Charms Bar*, introduced in Windows 8/8.1 and shown here in part on the right.

Please Note:

In this book, *Start Menu* includes both the more traditional menu on the left of the screen, shown on pages 8 and 9 and also the tiled area, which is re-sizeable in Windows 10. (Except in Windows 10 *Tablet mode* where Start again occupies the full screen).

More New Features in Windows 10

The next few pages briefly outline some more of the new features in Windows 10.

Continuum

This feature in Windows 10 detects what sort of computer you are using and configures Windows 10 accordingly. If you're using a laptop or desktop computer, the Start Menu and Taskbar will be displayed as shown on pages 8 and 9, suitable for use with a mouse and keyboard. If using a touchscreen tablet or smartphone, *Continuum* will detect this and *Tablet mode* will be selected, with the tiled Start area occupying the whole screen, similar to those shown on pages 6 and 7 for Windows 8.

Universal Apps

Windows 10 has been designed so that it uses the same *common core* of coding i.e. program instructions, on all of the different types of computer platform, i.e. laptop, desktop, 2-in-1 hybrid computer, tablet, smartphone and other Windows 10 devices such as the Xbox console.

In the past, versions of Windows were not the same for different devices such as desktop computers and smart phones. Now with Windows 10 being basically the same across all of the different computer platforms, it's easier to create *Universal Apps*. This means a user can experience the same apps with the same look and feel on any of their devices. Whether using a phone, tablet, laptop or desktop computer *the same app is installed for each type of device from the same app Store*. Obviously the development of universal apps is ongoing and some apps have not yet been updated for this capability. An example of a universal app is the photo editing program, Adobe Photoshop Express, shown below in the Store in Windows 10.

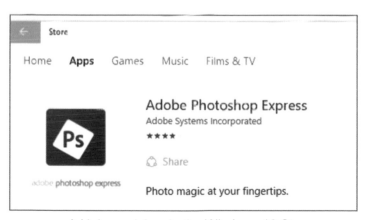

A Universal App in the Windows 10 Store

Cortana

This is a ***virtual assistant*** or ***personal digital assistant*** in Windows 10. Cortana appears as a search bar at the bottom left of the screen, where you can *type* your search criteria.

Or select the microphone and *speak* your request.

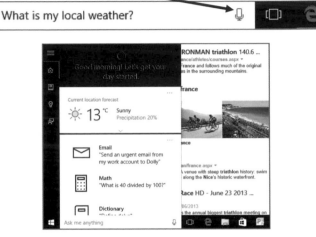

Cortana Virtual Assistant

The main functions of Cortana are:

- Searching for information, such as:
  "What's the weather in Cannes?"
  "What's 89 divided by 7?"
- Providing notifications and reminders.
- Providing latest information such as weather and traffic in ***your own location***.
- Sending e-mails you've dictated to Cortana.

Cortana is also available for iPads and iPhones and Android tablets and smartphones.

Microsoft Edge

This is the new Web browser for Windows 10. The previous Windows browser, Internet Explorer is still available if you need to use it, as discussed later in this book.

Microsoft Edge has a number of built-in tools which allow you to write comments, highlight or draw on a Web page, then share a copy of the annotated page to a friend, by e-mail or social networking, etc.

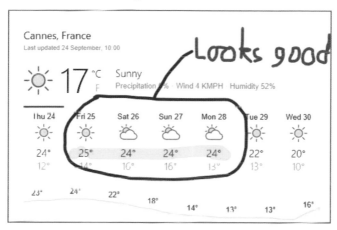

Microsoft Edge also works with Cortana, discussed on the previous page, enabling you to search using both typed and spoken search criteria. You can also search by typing your keywords into the Address bar at the top of the screen.

Another new feature in Microsoft Edge is *Reading view*. If you have pages of information which you want to read carefully or print on paper, Microsoft Edge removes all of the adverts and Web related material. This leaves just the printed document, like the pages in a book, without the clutter often present on Web pages.

The Action Centre

The Action Centre is launched by tapping the *Notification* icon in the bottom right of the screen, shown on the right and below. Notifications are operating system messages detailing events, problems and e-mails, as shown below.

Below the list of notifications is the Action Centre menu shown below. You can **Collapse** or **Expand** this menu.

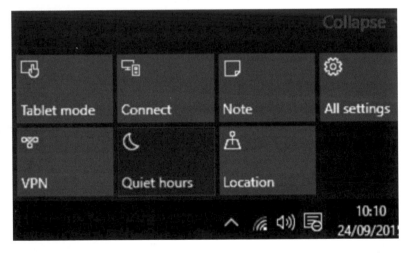

The **Tablet mode** tile on the menu above acts as a "toggle". When you tap or click the dark grey **Tablet mode** tile it changes to red, indicating that **Tablet mode** is now switched On. Tap or click again to switch **Tablet mode** Off and change the tile back to grey.

Tablet mode

Selecting **Tablet mode** (i.e. touchscreen mode), shown on the previous page, displays the Start tiles over the full screen, like Windows 8/8.1, as shown on pages 6 and 7. The Taskbar along the bottom of the screen, shown on pages 8 and 9 is also removed in **Tablet mode**.

Connect

This feature is used to connect your computer to the Internet, e.g. via a *WiFi* router, or to a *Bluetooth* device.

Note

This launches the OneNote app used for keeping notes and pictures. OneNote is discussed in detail later.

All settings

This is like the Control Panel in earlier versions of Windows, where you can change personal settings, preferences, security and accounts and set up devices, etc. **All settings** is also accessible from the Start Menu.

VPN

This is used to set up a *Virtual Private Network* of computers. This might involve, say connecting a company's own network to a public network such as the Internet.

Quiet hours

When this is On, sounds from notifications, such as the arrival of an e-mail, are switched off during set times.

Location

This switches Location services On or Off. Some apps need location services to give you local information such as weather, traffic news or lists of nearby restaurants.

Key Points: The Evolution of Windows 10

- The *Start Menu*, omitted in Windows 8/8.1, returns at the request of mouse/keyboard users.

- *Start* is now an array of tiles and part of the Start Menu, which can be re-sized and scrolled.

- *Tablet mode* for touchscreens displays the Start tiles full-screen - similar to Windows 8/8.1 on page 7.

- So Windows 10 now caters for both traditional mouse/keyboard users as well as touchscreen users.

- The *Cortana* personal assistant uses voice and typed search criteria, answers questions, gives local information and displays reminders.

- The *Microsoft Edge* browser allows you to add notes or highlights to a Web page and send a copy to a friend. Edge works closely with Cortana.

- *Reading view* in Microsoft Edge strips away any adverts, etc., to display a clear, uncluttered Web document.

- *Continuum* detects whether you're using a traditional mouse and keyboard or a touchscreen device. Then Cortana switches on either Tablet mode or the new Start Menu (pages 8 and 9).

- *Universal apps*, all obtainable from one app *Store*, can run on all platforms — laptop, desktop, 2-in-1, tablet and smartphone.

- The *Action Centre* displays notifications and gives access to various settings, including Tablet mode. The *Chimes* icons in Windows 8/8.1 are not present in Windows 10.

2

Getting Set Up

Obtaining Windows 10

All of the reviews suggest that Windows 10 will be a very popular operating system and a really worthwhile upgrade. There are several ways you can obtain Windows 10:

- If you already have a computer running Windows 7 or Windows 8/8.1, there is a free upgrade which can be downloaded from the Internet to your computer.

- Or you can buy a new computer with Windows 8/8.1 installed, then download the Windows 10 upgrade.

- Or buy a new computer with Windows 10 already installed.

- The free upgrade is not available for versions of the Windows operating system earlier than Windows 7, such as Windows XP.

- Users of earlier versions such as Windows XP need to buy a copy of Windows 10 and do a *clean install* from a DVD or from an Internet download.

These methods are discussed in more detail shortly. However, before upgrading an existing computer, you should check that it meets the minimum specification for Windows 10, as discussed on the next page.

Minimum Specification for Windows 10

Processor: 1 gigahertz (GHz) or faster

RAM: 1 gigabyte (GB) for 32-bit or 2GB for 64-bit

Hard Drive: 16GB for 32-bit or 20GB for 64-bit

Graphics: DirectX9 or later

Display: 800x600

Checking Your Computer's Upgrade Status

If you are using a modern machine already running Windows 8/8.1 then it will probably already meet the minimum specification listed above. You can check its specification as shown below.

Right-click the **Get Windows 10** icon, on the right-hand side of the Taskbar at the bottom of the screen, as shown on the right. Now select **Check your upgrade status** as shown below.

> Get Windows 10
>
> Check your upgrade status
>
> Go to Windows Update
>
> Learn about Windows 10

The screenshot at the top of the next page shows the results of checking a Windows 7 laptop. This met all of the requirements to run Windows 10.

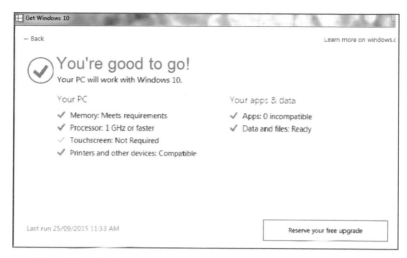

Checking that a computer meets Windows 10 requirements

The specification for Windows 10 is not too demanding by modern standards. However, if you have a machine which doesn't meet the requirements, it may be worth bringing it up to date with some new components. For example, if you don't have enough space on your hard drive you could move some of your files (documents and photos, etc.) onto external storage such as a removable *flash drive* or an *SSD* (*Solid State Drive*). These devices are easy to connect to a USB port on the computer. (Copying and managing files is discussed in Chapter 11).

If you have a desktop or laptop computer which doesn't have enough memory or RAM required for Windows 10, as shown at the top of page 18, it should be possible to add some extra memory modules.

If you are new to computing, it may be advisable to seek the advice of a reputable local computer shop or expert, before trying to modify an older computer yourself.

Basic Information About Your Computer

You can find out quite a lot about a computer running an earlier version of Windows, such as Windows 7. The following information is displayed after selecting **Start/Control Panel/System and Security/ System**.

View basic information about your computer

Windows edition

Windows 7 Home Premium

Copyright © 2009 Microsoft Corporation. All rights reserved.

Service Pack 1
Get more features with a new edition of Windows 7

System

Manufacturer:	Acer
Model:	Aspire V5-531
Rating:	**4.3** Windows Experience Index
Processor:	Intel(R) Pentium(R) CPU 967 @ 1.30GHz 1.30 GHz
Installed memory (RAM):	4.00 GB (3.80 GB usable)
System type:	64-bit Operating System

The information above was from a Windows 7 laptop, running Windows Home Premium. With Service Pack 1 (SP1) installed, it's ready for the free upgrade to Windows 10 Home, as shown on page 23. You can also see that it's currently running the 64-bit version of Windows 7, so the 64-bit version of Windows 10 should be compatible. The 1.3 GHz processor exceeds the minimum 1.0GHz required by Windows 10, as shown on page 18.

Finally you can see that the 4GB of RAM is more than the 2GB Windows 10 minimum. This will exploit the speed of the 64-bit processor and the 64-bit version of Windows 10.

32-bit or 64-bit Versions of Windows 10

Most modern computers are described as having a *32-bit* or *64-bit processor*. Data and information in a computer is represented entirely by 0's and 1's, or *binary digits*, usually referred to as *bits* for short. So a computer designed for 64-bits can handle instructions and data in bigger "chunks" and therefore faster than a 32-bit computer. (Earlier microcomputers had only 8-bit or 16-bit *architecture* (i.e. design) and were therefore much slower).

Windows 10 is available in 32-bit and 64-bit versions. If you have a 32-bit computer, you won't be able to run the 64-bit version of Windows 10.

If you upgrade your computer to Windows 10 using the free Internet download, the correct version of Windows 10, 32-bit or 64-bit, will be automatically selected then downloaded and installed on your machine.

However, if you have a computer running a version of Windows earlier than Windows 7, you will to have buy a copy of Windows 10 from a retailer. This may be supplied on a flash drive or DVD and you will have to choose which version to install. Some points to consider are:

- A computer with a 32-bit processor will not run the 64-bit version of Windows 10.

- A computer with less than 4MB of RAM will not benefit from using the 64-bit version of Windows 10.

- A 64-bit computer can still run the 32-bit version of Windows 10. If you need to run a lot of earlier 32-bit applications software, it may be better to install the 32-bit version of Windows 10, even on a computer capable of running the 64-bit version.

Windows 10 Editions

As with previous versions of Windows, there are several different editions of Windows 10 designed for various categories of user:

Windows 10 Home

This is the consumer edition for users of laptop, desktop, tablet and 2-in-1 computers.

Windows 10 Pro

Similar to Windows 10 Home, but with extra features for the professional and small business user.

Windows 10 Enterprise

This edition is designed for larger organisations and has extra emphasis on security and protection of information.

Windows 10 Education

Building on Windows 10 Enterprise, this edition is aimed at school and college staff and students and is available through volume licensing.

Windows 10 Mobile

This is designed for smartphones and small tablets and has all the basic features of Windows 10 Home.

Windows 10 Mobile Enterprise

Businesses can obtain this edition for smartphones and small tablets through volume licensing.

The edition of Windows 10 you receive from the free upgrade depends on the edition of Windows 7 or Windows 8/8.1 currently installed on your computer, as follows:

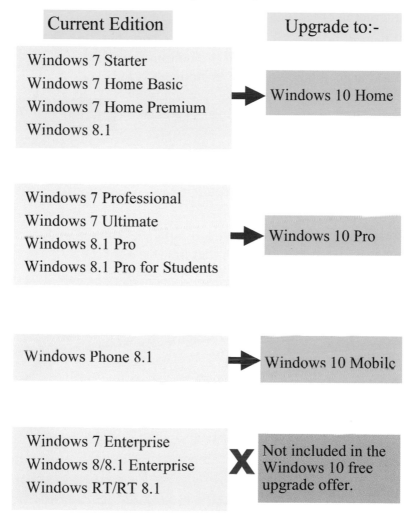

Current Edition	Upgrade to:-
Windows 7 Starter Windows 7 Home Basic Windows 7 Home Premium Windows 8.1	Windows 10 Home
Windows 7 Professional Windows 7 Ultimate Windows 8.1 Pro Windows 8.1 Pro for Students	Windows 10 Pro
Windows Phone 8.1	Windows 10 Mobile
Windows 7 Enterprise Windows 8/8.1 Enterprise Windows RT/RT 8.1	Not included in the Windows 10 free upgrade offer.

Installing Windows 10 as a Free Upgrade

This method of upgrading only applies to Windows 7 and Windows 8/8.1. Your computer must be connected to the Internet in order to download the upgrade.

When Windows 10 is available to you, the **Get Windows 10** icon appears at the bottom right of the Taskbar in Windows 7 and Windows 8/8.1. If your computer is eligible for the free upgrade, you can click the icon and select **Reserve your free upgrade**.

The upgrade is made available at different times in different locations and you may have to wait a while depending on the demand. You are notified when your Windows 10 upgrade is available.

You are given the chance to upgrade immediately or schedule the upgrade for another time.

Switch Off 3rd Party Security Software

Temporarily disable any 3rd party *firewall, anti-virus* and other security software. This can be done within the security app, which usually appears as an icon on the right of the Taskbar at the bottom of the screen. After installing Windows 10 the security features should be switched on again. This topic is also discussed on the next page.

Downloading the Windows 10 Files

First the files have to be downloaded from the Internet. Then you have a chance to schedule the upgrade or **Start the upgrade now**, as shown below.

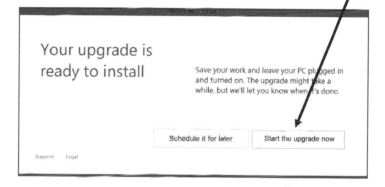

The upgrade may take up to two hours, depending on the speed of your equipment. Once the upgrade is complete you should be able to use your computer and all of its apps and settings straightaway. Although there are new features in Windows 10 such as the Cortana digital assistant and the Microsoft Edge Web browser, the basic methods of operation are similar to earlier versions of Windows. The Start Menu and Desktop in Windows 10 should seem familiar to users of earlier systems such as Windows 7 and XP. The tablet mode in Windows 10 is virtually the same as the Start Screen in Windows 8/8.1.

Installation Errors

As mentioned earlier, the first three installations I carried out went smoothly. The machines involved were a Windows 8.1 Desktop, a Windows 8.1 laptop and a Windows 7 laptop. It was simply a case of clicking the **Start the upgrade now** button and waiting. Downloading the Windows files took about 25 minutes and the installation took about an hour. During this time the computer re-started several times. After each installation I was able to use each computer as before — all apps, settings and device drivers worked without problems.

However, when I tried to install Windows 10 on a new 2-in-1 hybrid computer running Windows 8.1, the upgrade failed, with the error message **8024402C**. This error appears when a *security program* blocks access to the Internet. Such programs include *firewalls* and *antivirus programs*. The machines which upgraded successfully were running Windows' own Firewall and Defender security apps. The new machine which failed was pre-installed with a 3rd party antivirus and security package.

The solution is to *temporarily* disable any 3rd party security software before starting the upgrade. However, my second attempt to install Windows 10 on the new machine also failed, this time with the error **8020056**. This was caused by the debris left behind from the first unsuccessful download. The solution to this was to delete all of the downloaded upgrade files from the folder:-

C:\Windows\SoftwareDistribution\Download

(Managing and deleting files is discussed in Chapter 11).

The installation of Windows 10 then worked perfectly.

The Clean Install

If you're using an older version of Windows (earlier than Windows 7, such as Windows XP, Windows Vista and Windows RT) or the Enterprise versions listed on page 23, these are not eligible for the free upgrade to Windows 10. Instead you'll have to buy a copy of Windows 10, on a flash drive, DVD or pay for an Internet download of the software. Then you need to carry out a *clean install*. This completely wipes your hard disc of all software and all of your data files such as documents, photos, music, etc. Settings such as your Internet connection and e-mail accounts will also be lost. Also your *device drivers*, i.e. software needed to connect devices such as printers to your computer, will be removed.

So you need to *back up* all of your important files, including documents like reports, spreadsheets and irreplaceable collections of photos. This involves copying the files to a separate storage medium such as a flash drive or (more securely) a *read only* CD/DVD. You will also need to re-install any of the software or apps you've bought and installed previously. For this you'll need the original CD/DVDs or other media. Some device drivers are available from within Windows 10.

Carrying out a clean install of Windows 10 and reinstalling all of your own apps and data files is a complex task. If you're new to computing it would be advisable to ask a computer shop or a friend with the expertise to do the work. Alternatively you could buy a new machine with Windows 8.1 or Windows 10 already installed. A new Windows 8.1 machine can be freely upgraded to Windows 10 as discussed earlier.

Buying a New Computer

There is a range of devices capable of running Windows 10, from laptops and desktops, all-in-one computers to tablets and smartphones. (An *all-in-one* is a desktop computer with the main components integrated within the monitor).

Windows 10 has been designed to embrace both touchscreen operation for tablets, smartphones and all-in-one computers and desktop mode for mouse and keyboard operation with laptops and desktops. The *2-in-1* or *hybrid* computer such as the Microsoft Surface Pro 3 has a detachable keyboard. With the keyboard removed the device is used as a touchscreen tablet. With the keyboard attached the device is used like a laptop and you may also connect a mouse. The *Continuum* feature in Windows 10 detects whether or not the keyboard is attached and gives you a choice to select either tablet or desktop mode.

A Toshiba 2-in-1 computer with detachable keyboard, which can operate either as a laptop or as a touchscreen tablet

At the time of writing, new machines are being supplied with Windows 8.1 pre-installed but with a free upgrade to Windows 10 available as a download.

Laptop and 2-in-1 machines start of at around £150 while some all-in-one desktop computers are over £1000.

Setting Up Your Microsoft Account

If you buy a new computer with either Windows 8.1 or Windows 10 installed, you'll be able to *sign in* with an existing *Microsoft Account* or *sign up* for a new one. You normally log in to your account with your e-mail address and a suitable password.

You can create a new Microsoft Account at any time — not just during the initial setting up process. The Microsoft Account is used to log on to your computer at the start of a session. It can also be used as your Outlook.com e-mail address and as your identification on important services like OneDrive ("cloud" computing), Skype Internet telephone calls and the Windows Store for downloading apps.

To access the accounts on your computer, tap the Start button shown on the right, at the bottom left of the screen. Then select **Settings** from the Start Menu shown below.

From the **Settings** window which opens, select **Accounts** and then select **Add a Microsoft account**.

If you have a Microsoft Account, enter your e-mail address and password, then select **Sign in**. Otherwise select **Create One** next to **No account?** Then create and enter a new e-mail address and password, as shown below.

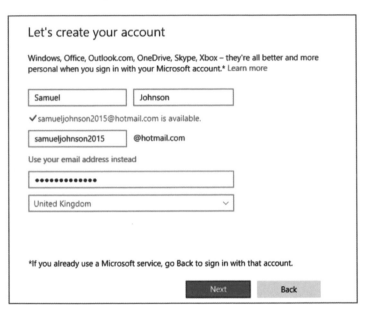

Your Account Picture

You can add a picture to your account. Select **Browse** shown on the right to use an existing photo saved on your computer or on a flash drive or camera card, etc. Alternatively, if you have a built-in camera or a Web cam, select **Camera** shown on the right to take a new picture for your account. Your picture will appear on the e-mails you send.

Your picture

Browse

Create your picture

Camera

Connecting to the Internet

If you upgrade an existing machine running either Windows 8/8.1 or Windows 7, your Internet connection will remain intact. With a new machine, you'll need to set up a new connection. This may involve obtaining a *wireless router*, which is normally supplied free when you subscribe to an Internet Service Provider such as BT.

Windows 10 will detect any nearby routers including your own and any of your neighbours' devices (e.g. **whitebox** shown on the right below). These can be viewed after selecting the Internet icon, shown on the right, in the Notification Area at the bottom right of the screen. Select your own router (e.g. **BTHub4r-9QXS**) from the list and enter the *wireless key* or password, normally found on the back of the router.

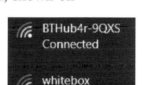

Setting Up a Printer

From the Start Menu select **Settings** and then **Devices** as shown on the right. Then after selecting **Add a printer or scanner**, the computer will search for any printers which are  connected. If a printer is detected, Windows will try to find and install the necessary driver software. Or you may be asked to install a disc containing the necessary software. Then your printer will be listed under **Printers**.

Now select **Devices and printers** to open the Control Panel and right-click over your printer and select **Set as default printer**. This adds a green tick to the image of your printer in the Control Panel, as shown on the right.

Key Points: Getting Set Up

- The free upgrade to Windows 10 only applies to Windows 8/8.1 and Windows 7.

- The free upgrade requires an Internet connection and preserves all of your settings, software and data files.

- Users of other versions of Windows must *buy* Windows 10 and carry out a lengthy *clean install*.

- This deletes all your software and files. These should be *backed up* before upgrading and restored later.

- There are several editions of Windows 10 including Home, Pro, Enterprise, Education and Mobile.

- A computer must meet a minimum technical specification in order to run Windows 10.

- It may be possible to improve an older computer by adding extra memory or freeing up disc space, etc.

- There are 32-bit and 64-bit versions of Windows 10. A 32-bit computer can't run the 64-bit Windows 10.

- New computers are currently supplied with Windows 8.1 with a free option to upgrade to Windows 10.

- Security software such as *firewalls* and *anti-virus* programs may stop the installation of Windows 10.

- To overcome this problem, the security software can be *temporarily* disabled, then switched on again.

- To save space on the hard drive, etc., you might later decide to delete your previous version of Windows.

Exploring Windows 10

Introduction

This chapter describes some of the main features of Windows 10. As discussed earlier, Windows 10 can be operated in the *Desktop* using the traditional mouse and physical keyboard. Or if you have a touchscreen device, you may prefer *Tablet mode* using touch *gestures* with your finger or a pen-like *stylus*.

The Windows 10 Desktop

Although the Windows 10 Desktop was designed for operation with a mouse and keyboard, if you have a touchscreen device you can still control the Desktop using touch gestures, if you prefer.

The Windows 10 Tablet Mode

A device running in the Tablet mode can also be controlled by a mouse. As discussed shortly, it's easy to switch between the Desktop and Tablet mode.

Desktop vs Tablet Mode

In general, if you're using a traditional laptop or desktop computer, you'll use it in the Windows Desktop together with a mouse and keyboard. Users of touchscreen devices such as tablets, smartphones and some all-in-one devices, will probably prefer touch operation. (Although physical keyboards are available for some touchscreen devices such as tablets and smartphones).

2-in-1 devices with detachable keyboards are designed to operate in either Desktop or Tablet mode. The 2-in-1 device can switch on the appropriate mode when the keyboard is either connected or detached, as discussed later.

Mouse Operations

Click

Press the left mouse button to select an object on the screen at the current cursor position, such as a menu option. Also click to open an app from a tile on the Start feature.

Double-click

Two left clicks in quick succession to open a folder in the File Explorer. Also launches an app from an icon.

Right-click

Press the right mouse button to open a shortcut or *context sensitive* menu. These menus list options relevant to the current cursor position.

Drag

Click over a screen object, then keeping the left button held down, drag the object to a new position, before releasing the left button. Can be used to change the position of a tile on Start or move a file or folder to a different folder in the File Explorer. Drag is also used to move horizontal or vertical *scroll bars* to advance forwards or backwards through a long document or window.

Scroll Wheel

This wheel, located in the centre of a mouse, is used to scroll through a long document on the screen.

Ctrl + Scroll Wheel

Hold down the Ctrl key and turn the scroll wheel. This zooms in or out of whatever is currently displayed on the screen.

Touchscreen Gestures

Tap

Press quickly but gently on the screen to launch an app from a tile on the Start area, or select an option from a menu.

Double-tap

Two quick taps to open a folder or flash drive, etc., in Windows File Explorer. A folder can also be opened by holding then releasing and selecting **Open** from the menu which pops up.

Hold and Release

Keep your finger gently pressing against an object or area of the screen for a few seconds then release to display a shortcut menu relevant to the current screen location.

Drag

Keeping your finger over a screen object such as a Start tile or a file in the File Explorer, move your finger over the screen and release to drop the object in its new location.

Swipe

This involves sliding your finger across the screen, usually from one of the edges. Swiping has many uses for displaying running apps and options and these are discussed in detail shortly.

Pinch or **Stretch** (move two fingers together or apart) to zoom out or zoom in.

Select will be used from now on to mean "click with a mouse" or "tap with a finger or stylus".

The Start Menu

Select the Start button, shown on the right, at the bottom left of the screen. Or press the Windows key on the keyboard. The Start Menu opens as shown below.

The Windows 10 Start Menu and Start tiles

The top part of the left-hand panel shown above lists your most used apps or programs. Select any of these to revisit the app, including listings of any previous documents, files or Web pages you've been working on.

The bottom left-hand side of the Start Menu shown below includes several very important features.

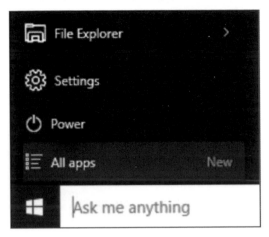

The Bottom of the Start Menu

Next to the Start button itself at the bottom left is the Cortana Search bar, into which you can type any question or search criteria you like. Or select the microphone icon as shown on the right below.

Then speak your request. You may need to train Cortana to recognise your voice in **Settings/Speech** discussed later in this book.

Select the microphone and say, "Tell me a joke."

The File Explorer

Selecting **File Explorer** shown at the top of the previous page displays your files and folders.

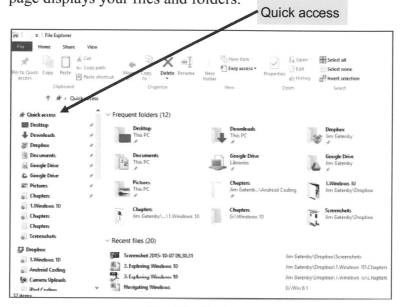

The File Explorer

The File Explorer is where you can organise all of your documents, photos, accounts, music, videos, etc., into a hierarchy of *folders*. The File Explorer also helps you to manage your storage devices such as hard drives, flash drives, CDs and external disc drives. **Quick access** in Windows 10 is a new feature which lists the files you've been recently working on and the folders you've been using frequently.

The File Explorer enables you to *create new folders* and *copy, move, delete* and *rename* files and folders.

Settings

Selecting **Settings** on the Start Menu shown on page 38 opens the window shown below. This is similar to the Control Panel in earlier versions of Windows. (The Control Panel is still available in Windows 10).

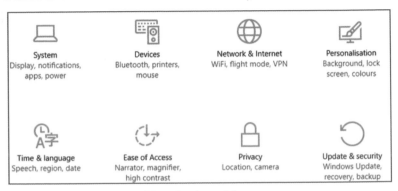

The Settings Menu

The Settings feature allows you to make many important changes and adjustments to your computer, such as personalising the display, setting up printers, etc., managing your Microsoft account and checking your computer's security and your connection to the Internet.

Update & security shown above and on the right is an important feature, allowing you to check your latest Windows updates. Updates may be to improve security and on Windows 10 they are installed automatically. *Windows Defender* protects against *malware* and *viruses*.

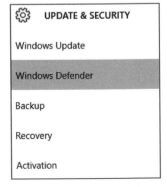

Power

Selecting **Power** on the Start Menu shown on page 37 and 38 displays the options **Sleep, Shut down** and **Restart**, as shown on the right. Sleep saves your work and puts the computer in a low power state. To wake it up, tap a key, move a mouse, etc.

Shut down shown on the right above turns the computer off. Before shutting down you should save any work and close any apps that are running.

Restart is often needed after installing new apps and can sometimes help to solve a problem.

All apps

Selecting this option on the Start Menu shown above and on page 37 opens the All apps menu shown below.

All apps menu   Tiles on Start

All of your apps or programs are listed down the left-hand panel, as shown on the previous page and below.

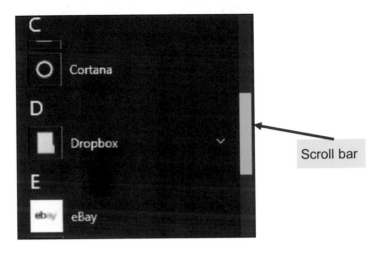

Scroll bar

Drag the scroll bar to browse through the list to search for a particular app. Or tap on any of the letter headings such as **D** shown above, then select the first letter of the app you are looking for.

So if you were looking for Python 2.7 for example, select any of the letter headings then tap P from the grid that appears as shown on the right.

This takes you straight to the **P** section of the All apps screen as shown below. Now select the required program, **Python 2.7**, as shown below, to open and run it on the screen.

.

If you right-click or tap and hold an app listed on the All apps menu, various options are displayed as shown on the right. **Pin to Start** means to create a new *tile* for the app on the Start feature discussed shortly.

Unpin from taskbar means to remove the icon for the app from the Taskbar along the bottom of the screen.

Apps on the Windows 10 Taskbar

Uninstall shown on the right above means to remove the app completely from your computer.

Tiles on the Start Menu

Tiles were introduced in Windows 8 and were known as the *Start Screen*, as they filled the whole screen and there was no Taskbar along the bottom. In Windows 10 the tiled area is much smaller by default and is now part of the Start Menu. The tiled area can be resized by dragging its edges vertically and horizontally.

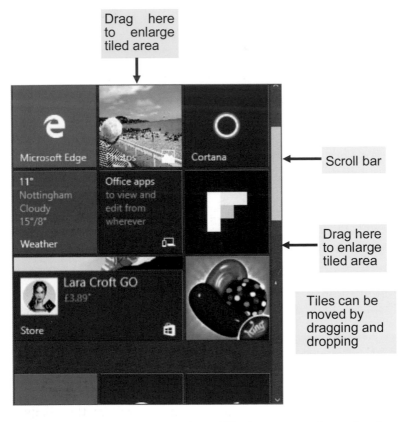

The tiles can be expanded to fill the screen by selecting **Tablet mode** in the Action Centre as described on page 14.

Managing Tiles

If you scroll around the Start Menu tiles, you'll see that they represent a variety of features. Some tiles are used to launch apps such as the **Microsoft Edge** browser, shown on the right and on the previous page.

Other tiles are "live" and display constantly changing information such as the news headlines or weather. Select the tile to get the full-screen information

Right-click or press and hold a tile such as the **Mail** tile shown on the right. **Resize** shown on the right offers four different tile sizes. **Pin to taskbar** places an icon for the app on the Taskbar at the bottom of the screen.

The **Mail** app is shown as a tile to the right and as an icon on the Taskbar as shown below on the right.

Turn live tile off shown above on the right stops the display of constantly changing information on a tile such as news headlines and weather. The tile is then just a link to the information displayed on the full screen.

Creating Your Own Start Menu Tiles

Apart from apps, a tile can be used as a quick way to open folders containing documents or photos, etc., or a frequently used Web site.

For example, I have a folder in the ***Dropbox*** cloud storage system, for all the chapters in this book.

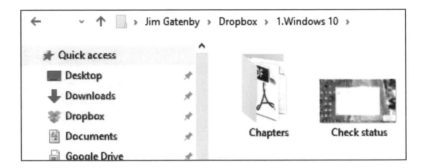

Right-click or hold over the folder icon for **Chapters** shown above then select **Pin to Start** from the menu which appears. The new tile for **Chapters** appears in Start Menu alongside of two other tiles I've created.

To create a tile for a Web page, open the page in Microsoft Edge as discussed later. Then select the 3-dot menu button shown on the right,  at the top right of Microsoft Edge and select **Pin to Start** from the drop-down menu.

The Start Tiles in Tablet Mode

If you're using a touchscreen tablet or smartphone, or touchscreen 2-in-1 or all-in-one computer, you'll probably want to use Tablet mode as shown below. (You can also use Tablet mode with a mouse and keyboard if that's what you prefer).

The full screen Start tiles in Tablet mode

As shown above, the tiles in the Start Menu now take up most of the screen, unlike the reduced area when the tiles are part of the Start Menu. In the traditional Desktop mode, icons for apps that you've pinned to the Taskbar or apps you're are currently running are displayed on the Taskbar, as shown at the bottom of page 45. However, in Tablet mode, as shown above, by default these icons are not displayed on the Taskbar. However, this is the default setting and the program icons can be displayed if you prefer, as discussed on page 49.

Tablet Mode Settings

To switch Tablet mode On, from the Start Menu, select Settings, as shown on page 38. Then drag the button, shown below under **Tablet mode**, to the **On** position.

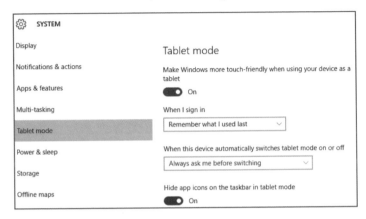

Windows 10 Tablet mode settings

The Continuum Feature in Windows 10

A 2-in-1 computer, i.e. with a detachable keyboard, can be used either as a tablet or as a laptop. If you detach or attach the keyboard, *Continuum* automatically selects the correct mode. As shown above and below you can set Windows 10 to ask you before switching to or from Tablet mode.

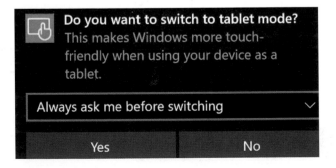

Another quick way to switch Tablet mode On or Off is using the Action Centre, shown on page 14. This is opened by selecting its icon in the Notification Area on the right of the Windows Taskbar at the bottom right of the screen.

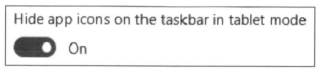

There is also an option in **Settings/System/Tablet mode** to hide the apps icons on the Taskbar (shown on page 45), when the Tablet mode is **On**, as shown below.

Hide app icons on the taskbar in tablet mode

On

Tablet mode introduces a few new buttons of its own:

This button, in the top left-hand corner of the Tablet mode screen, displays the Start Menu, as shown to the left of the tiles on page 37.

Opens a menu with the options **Sleep**, **Shut down** and **Restart** as shown on page 41.

Opens the All apps menu shown on pages 41 and 42.

Displays the previous screen.

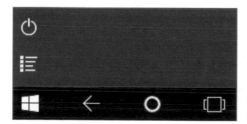

The above three icons, also shown on the left, are discussed elsewhere in this book.

Key Points: Exploring Windows 10

• Windows 10 can be used in the traditional Desktop designed for mouse and keyboard or in Tablet mode, designed for touchscreen tablets and smartphones.

• The Desktop launches apps from the *Start Menu*. Tablet mode uses *tiles* on a full screen *Start* feature.

• The Start Menu lists your most used apps and displays the All apps feature listing all your apps.

• The Start menu gives access to the **File Explorer**, used to manage all your files, folders and disc drives.

• The **Settings** feature in the Start Menu allows you to make major adjustments to your computer.

• The **Power** button in the Start Menu has options to **Shut down**, **Restart** or put your computer to **Sleep**.

• The Start Menu includes an adjustable tiled area which can be increased and decreased by dragging.

• Tiles can also be used to launch Web pages and display live information such as news and weather.

• You can create your own tiles, resize or delete tiles and move them by dragging and dropping.

• The Continuum feature detects what type of system you are using (mouse or touchscreen) and gives you a choice between Tablet mode and the Desktop.

• In Tablet mode there are icons allowing you to access the Start Menu and the All apps menu.

The Desktop in Detail

Apps on the Desktop

The Desktop is the launch pad for much of what you do on Windows 10. After you install Windows 10 or buy a new computer, many important apps and features are already installed on the Desktop. As shown below, these default apps appear as *icons* on the Start Menu on the left-hand side of the screen and as *tiles* on the Start area. There also icons on the Taskbar at the bottom of the screen and *shortcut* icons on the Desktop background.

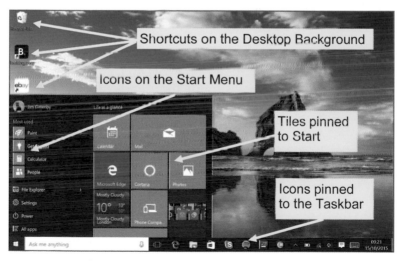

Standard icons and tiles on the Desktop

Obtaining an App from the Store

In addition to the default or standard apps provided on a new installation of Windows 10, as shown on the previous page, you can obtain apps of your own choice from the many thousands available in the Store in Windows 10. Apps in the Store should have been thoroughly checked and approved by Microsoft, so there should be no risk of *viruses* or *malware* (malicious software). This can be a risk when installing software from unknown sources.

In this example, the free *Google* app will be installed from the Windows 10 Store. Although Windows 10 has its own well-established Bing search program within Cortana, Google is the most popular *search engine* in the world. As a result the verb "to Google" is now in common use. Also, when you install Google, you get several other free Google apps such as Gmail, Maps, YouTube, Drive (cloud storage) and Photos.

Finding an App in the Windows Store

The Windows 10 Store has many thousands of apps, many of them free. To open the Store, select its icon on the Taskbar at the bottom of the screen.

Then enter **Google** in the Search bar at the top right of the Store window.

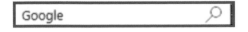

Some of the results of the search are shown below. The main (free) Google app is shown on the left.

Free

Installing an App

Select **Free** shown above and then select **Install** to download and save Google on your computer. Then select **Open** to launch the Google app ready for use.

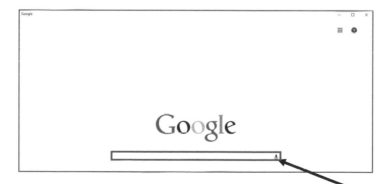

The search bar at the bottom of the Google window above is used to type in your search *keywords*. Or select the microphone icon and speak the keywords.

Apps Automatically Pinned to the Start Menu

When you install an app such as Google from the Store, an icon for the app is automatically pinned to the Start Menu, under **Recently added** as shown below.

The new Google icon added to the Start Menu

Right-click or hold then release over the Google icon to display the menu (**Pin to Start**, etc.,) shown above.

Creating a Tile for the New App on Start

Pin to Start shown above creates a tile for Google on Windows 10 Start shown in the extract on the right. Click or tap this tile to quickly launch and run the Google app.

Deleting a Tile from Start

Right-click or hold and release over the tile, then select **Unpin from Start**, as shown on the right.

Pinning an Icon for the New App on the Taskbar

Pin to taskbar on the menu shown at the top of the previous page places an icon for the Google app on the Taskbar at the bottom of the Desktop, as shown on the right and below.

Click or tap to launch the app and start using it.

Unpinning an App from the Taskbar

Right-click the icon or hold and release the icon, then select **Unpin this program from taskbar** as shown below.

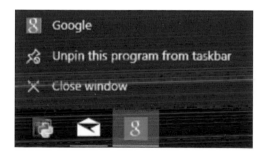

Please note that a number of apps are already pre-installed and have icons on the centre left of the Taskbar, as shown in the sample below.

The apps above, reading from left to right, are the Microsoft Edge browser, the File Explorer, the Store and Skype, the Internet telephone service.

Pinning an icon to the Taskbar shown on the previous page gives a quick way to launch your favourite apps with a single click or a tap. However, space on the Taskbar is limited, particularly on tablets and small 2-in-1 computers.

Creating a Desktop Shortcut for an App

Fortunately you can also use the main Desktop background screen as a launch pad for apps, as shown on page 51. This provides far more space for apps than on the Taskbar.

To create a shortcut for an *app* on the Windows 10 Desktop, locate the app in the Start Menu shown on page 51 or on the All apps menu, as shown on page 41. Then drag the icon for the app and drop it on a suitable part of the Desktop as shown below using the Google app.

To launch an app from the Desktop, double-click or double tap the icon. (Or right-click or hold and select **Open**).

Deleting a Shortcut Icon

To delete a shortcut icon, right-click or hold and release, then select **Delete** from the menu. This doesn't uninstall the app from your computer, it simply removes the icon from the Desktop. There is also an option to **Rename** a shortcut.

Creating a Desktop Shortcut for a Folder or File

To place a shortcut to an object such as a folder, file or photo, etc., right-click or hold and release over the object in the File Explorer. Then select **Create shortcut** from the menu which opens, as shown below. There is also another option, **Send to**, also shown below, which opens a menu with further options including **Desktop (create shortcut)**.

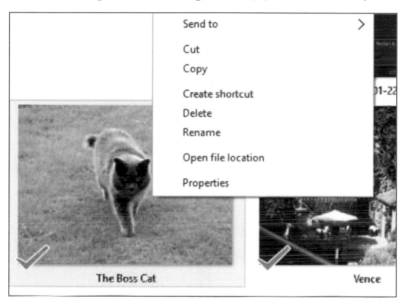

This places a shortcut icon for the photo on the Desktop, as shown below. Also shown is a shortcut to a folder containing part of the text of this book.

Double-click or double-tap the shortcut icon to open the folder, file or photo, etc.

Creating a Desktop Shortcut to a Web Page

This can be done in the *Internet Explorer*, the predecessor to Microsoft Edge and still available in Windows 10. In the Cortana Search bar at the bottom left of the Desktop, type "Open Internet Explorer".

Or tap or click the microphone icon and say "Open Internet Explorer". Internet Explorer opens as shown below.

With Internet Explorer open on the screen, enter the search keywords for the Web page you want in the Search Bar, as shown below.

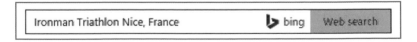

Cortana is a *personal assistant* with many other functions apart from searching as discussed above. Cortana is discussed in more detail in Chapter 7.

When you find the page you want right-click or hold over a *blank part* of the Web page borders to open the menu shown below on the right.

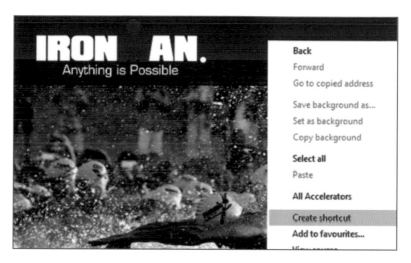

After selecting **Create shortcut**, shown on the menu above, tap or click **Yes** shown below.

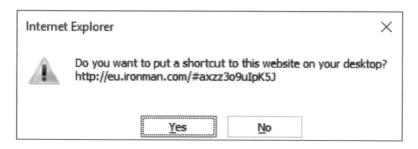

This places a shortcut icon for the Web site on the Desktop, as shown on the right. Double-click or double-tap to open the Web page.

Launching Apps

There are several alternative ways to launch an app:

- Select its name or icon on the Start Menu.
- Select its icon on the Taskbar.
- Select the *tile* for the app on Start.
- Double-click or double-tap its icon on the Desktop.

("Select" above means click or tap).

As an example, four different ways to launch the Python 2.7 coding app are shown below:

Start Menu option   Taskbar icon

Start menu tile   Desktop shortcut icon

Apps Currently Running

In the sample section of a Taskbar shown below, four apps are currently up and running in a computer. This is indicated by the four yellow lines under the icons shown below.

In the example on the previous page, the four running apps are, reading from left to right, the File Explorer, the Windows 10 Store, Microsoft Publisher and Windows Paint.

Apps which have not been pinned to the Taskbar, when launched from Start, the Start Menu or the Desktop will still appear on the Taskbar, but only while they are running.

Thumbnails on the Taskbar

Hover, i.e. hold the cursor, over an app on the Taskbar that is currently running, such as Internet Explorer shown on the right and below. A *thumbnail* or miniature version of the screen appears as shown below. Click the thumbnail to display the app full-screen or click the cross to close the app, in this example Internet Explorer, as shown on the right and below.

At the time of writing there is no touchscreen gesture equivalent to hovering the cursor with a mouse or touchpad. However, as discussed shortly, you can swipe in from the left to see all the apps currently running on a touchscreen.

If you are running an app such as a word processor, publisher or photo editor, you may have several documents open at the same time. Obviously, only one document can occupy the screen, while the others are hidden in the background.

The **Photos** app shown on the right and below currently has three files open. Click a thumbnail to see a photo, document or Web page full screen. Hover over a thumbnail and click the cross to close the photo, document, or Web page, etc.

Task View

Click or tap the Task View icon shown on the right and on the Taskbar below.

Alternatively, with a touchscreen, swipe in from the left-hand edge of the screen. Small versions of all of the apps or programs currently running are displayed, as shown at the top of the next page.

Windows key

Windows Key + Tab

Task View can also be opened by holding down the Windows key and pressing the Tab key.

Click or tap any of the apps to enlarge it, so that you can view it and perhaps edit a document, etc., on the full screen.

Task View is particularly useful if you use several different programs. You can see what's running and easily switch between them by clicking or tapping the one you want.

Alt+Tab

Another way to see what apps you're currently running and to switch between them is to hold down the Alt key and keep pressing the Tab key. This displays all of the current apps in a band across the screen, as shown below.

If you release the Alt key, the app currently highlighted by a white rectangle is opened on the full screen.

Virtual Desktops

This feature is part of Task View. Open Task View by clicking its icon on the Taskbar, as shown on the right. Initially you only have one desktop, but you can add more by clicking or tapping **New desktop** shown on the right and on the right of the Taskbar below.

As shown in the example below, two desktops are represented by thumbnails above the Taskbar.

Virtual Desktops

Each desktop can have several apps running. It's a bit like having several different computers running on one screen. You can switch between desktops by clicking the thumbnails, such as **Desktop 2** shown above.

Then click or tap the Task View icon shown at the top of this page to see what's running on that particular desktop.

Windows 10 Snap

This feature allows you to display several "live" windows on the screen at the same time. These are not just images of windows but fully operational apps in their own windows.

For example, you could read a report on a Web site on the Internet in Microsoft Edge in the left-hand window and write about the report using Microsoft Word, open in the right-hand window.

With software such as photo-editing, word processing, or spreadsheets, etc., having two windows open side by side also allows you to edit documents or cut and paste or drag and drop screen objects between the two windows.

The screenshot below shows a photo open in Windows Paint and a document open in Microsoft Publisher.

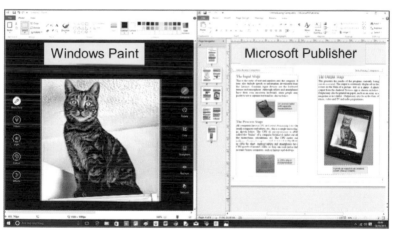

Two Apps Snapped Vertically

To return to the empty Desktop at any time, click or tap in the bottom right-hand corner of the screen.

Snapping Vertically

The method for snapping two windows vertically, similar to the example at the bottom of the previous page, is as follows:

- Click or tap the Task View icon shown on the right to display all of the apps currently running.
- Tap in the centre of one of the two required apps, such as Paint, to display it on the full screen.
- Drag the *title bar* of this first app to one edge of the screen. It snaps into place filling one half of the screen.
- The other apps will still be displayed in Task View as shown by the three smaller images below.

- Click or tap in the centre of the second app and it will snap into place to fill the second half of the screen, as shown at the top of the next page.

Snapping a window to the right or left of the screen can also be done using the Windows Logo Key, i.e.

⊞ + right or left arrow key

Opening Four Windows by Snapping

To open four windows on the screen simultaneously, drag the title bar of each window to a corner of the screen. You can continue to use all the features of each app as if they were occupying a full screen window of their own.

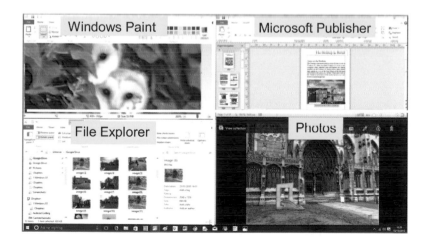

The Action Centre

This feature appears when you click or tap the **New notifications** icon on the right of the Taskbar shown on the right and below.

(The area of the Taskbar shown above is known as the System Tray and you can choose which icons appear on it, as discussed shortly.)

The Action Centre opens, as shown below.

The top half of the Action Centre lists any notifications you've received such as e-mails, software updates installed or messages from Facebook and Twitter.

The lower part of the Action Centre displays the Quick Action buttons. These are an easy way to access some important features, such as **Tablet mode**, **Connect** (your Internet connection) and **All settings**. The number of Quick Action buttons and their functions vary with different types of computer. For example, the **Flight mode** and **Battery saver** buttons will not appear on most desktop computers.

Some of the Quick Action buttons act as *toggles*, e.g. to switch **Tablet mode** on or off.

The **All settings** button shown on the previous page opens the **SETTINGS** window, partly shown below. Amongst many other things, this window can be used to control the notifications you receive and the icons which will appear on the Taskbar, as discussed on the next page.

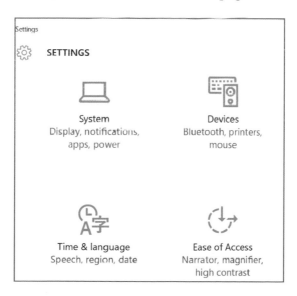

Click or tap **System** shown on the previous page and then select **Notifications & actions** from the menu which appears as shown below.

Under **Quick actions** shown above, after selecting each of the four icons in turn, you can choose, as shown below, which of the Quick Actions will occupy the top four positions in the Action Centre, as shown on page 68 under **Collapse**. In **Collapse** mode these are the only buttons seen.

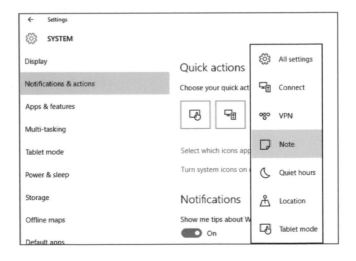

The **Notifications and Actions** window in **SYSTEM** also allows you select which apps will generate notifications.

Links on the **Notifications and Actions** window shown on the previous page allow you to select which icons appear on the Taskbar and to turn system icons on or off, as shown below.

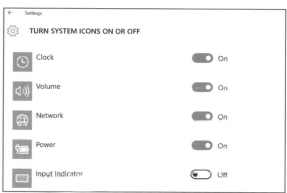

A typical System Tray is shown below. The icons for some apps can be *hidden*. These can be displayed by clicking or tapping the **Show hidden icons** button shown below.

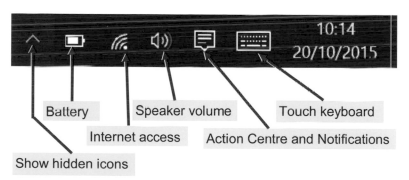

The icons displayed above depend on what is switched On or Off as shown in the **Settings** at the top of the page. Also, not all computers have batteries or touch keyboards.

Key Points: The Desktop in Detail

- The *Start Menu* can be used to launch all of the apps or programs on the computer. New apps which you install appear automatically on the Start Menu.

- Many apps are pre-installed and you can add others after downloading them from the *Store*.

- Icons for favourite apps can be pinned to the Taskbar at the bottom of the screen or added as *shortcuts* to the Desktop background.

- *Tiles* for apps, folders and Web pages can be added to the Start Menu.

- Apps currently running are shown underlined on the Taskbar and may also be viewed as *thumbnails*.

- *Task View* displays images of the apps currently running, so you can easily switch between them.

- *Virtual Desktops* allow you to have several desktops on one computer and switch between them. Each desktop can run several apps simultaneously.

- *Snapping* allows you to run two or more apps side by side on the screen, for the exchange of information.

- The *Action Centre* presents *notifications* of messages, updates, etc., and has *Quick Action* buttons for important tasks and settings.

- The *All settings* button can be used to tailor the notifications in the Action Centre and to select the icons displayed in the *System Tray* on the Taskbar.

Personalising Windows 10

Introduction

Although Windows 10 is ready to use as soon as the installation and initial setting up are complete, not all of the default settings may be to your liking. This chapter shows how you can use the settings in Windows 10 to make changes to suit your own needs and preferences.

The topics covered include:

- Changing the colour schemes and themes of the Desktop Background and the Lock Screen, including using your own photos.

- Setting up a *screen saver* to protect the computer while it's temporarily inactive.

- Using the low power consumption *sleep mode*.

- Setting the computer to open the Lock screen and require a password when returning from the sleep or screen saver modes.

- Using *hibernate* to save any open files before shutting down.

- Selecting the apps and folders which will appear on the Start Menu.

Personalising the Desktop

Tap the Start button shown on the right and then select **Settings** from the Start Menu. From the **SETTINGS** window which opens, select **Personalisation**. Down the left-hand side of the window shown below are several features which can be modified, i.e. **Background**, **Colours**, **Lock screen**, **Themes** and **Start**.

Personalisation
Background, lock
screen, colours

You'll probably spend a lot of time with the Desktop on display so you might want to customize it with your own picture or slide show.

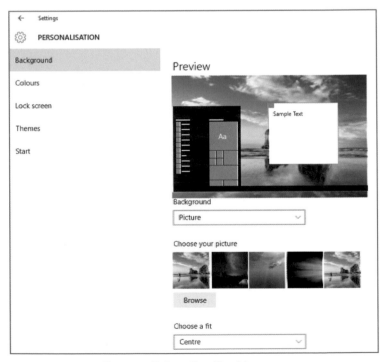

Personalising the Desktop

The **Picture** bar shown on the previous page has three options for the Desktop background

| Picture |
| Solid colour |
| Slideshow |

Picture can be used to insert one of the pictures provided in Windows 10.

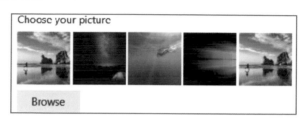

Or you can select **Browse** and look for your own picture on your hard drive, Internal Storage or perhaps a removable device such as a flash drive/memory stick or an SD camera card. When you've found the picture you want, select **Choose your picture** and your new desktop will be inserted as shown in the example below.

There is also an option to have a *slideshow* for the Desktop, as shown at the top of this page. In this case you browse for a photo *album* and set the amount of time before the picture is changed.

Using the Colours Option

This option on the **PERSONALISATION** menu shown on page 74 takes an *accent colour*, i.e. a bright colour, from your chosen Desktop background. This can then be used to colour other features on the screen such as Start and the Taskbar, depending on the settings chosen in the list shown below.

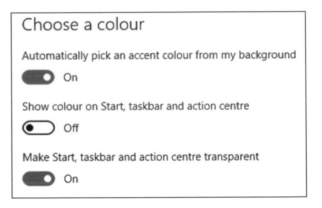

Personalising the Lock Screen

The Lock Screen is used to stop other people from using your computer without you knowing about it. The Lock Screen is the first full screen you see when the computer starts up. You normally click or tap the screen then enter a password before you can start using the computer.

It's also possible to secure a computer by displaying the Lock Screen when it "wakes up" after a period of inactivity in *sleep mode*. Similarly there is an option to display the Lock Screen and require a password after the computer has been running a *screen saver*. Sleep mode and screen savers are discussed shortly.

Open the **PERSONALISATION** window as described at the top of page 74 and select **Lock screen**, as shown on the left below.

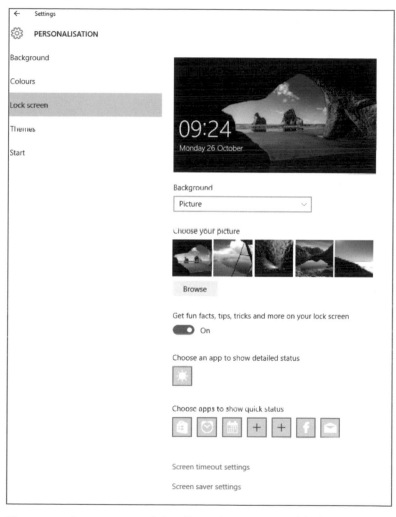

You can choose one of the five pictures provided or **Browse** your storage media for a suitable picture of your own.

Displaying Statuses on the Lock Screen

With the blue button shown below switched **On** you can set the Lock screen to display facts and tips, etc., in the form of *statuses* or updates and messages from selected apps.

Show detailed
statuses for
this app

Scroll to
see more
apps

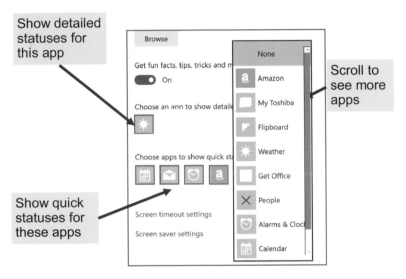

Show quick
statuses for
these apps

The upper icon shown above and on the right displays a *detailed status* for an app, in this case **Weather**. To change the app, tap over the square then select another app from the list of apps shown above. The lower row of apps shown above and on the right allows you to display a *quick status* for each of seven apps chosen from the list of apps. (As shown below you can select up to seven apps. The + sign means no app has been selected yet to fill this position).

Location

So, for example, you could set the Lock screen to display a detailed status of the weather in your area. (Your Location should be switched on by default, but if necessary this can be done in the **Location** option in the **PRIVACY** section of the main **Settings** menu shown on page 40.)

> When location services for this account are on, apps and services you allow can request location and location history.
>
> Location
>
> On

The Screen Saver

Early CRT (cathode Ray Tube) monitors were liable to damage if a computer was inactive for a long time with the same screen display. The *screen saver* is a program designed to prevent this by displaying constantly changing patterns or images when the computer is on but inactive.

Unlike *sleep mode*, discussed shortly, the screen saver is not a low power consumption mode since the computer is still working to display the moving patterns and images.

Modern computers with LCD monitors do not suffer the same *burn-in* problem, but screen savers are still used for entertainment, amusement and security.

The screen saver is useful if you regularly have to leave the computer unattended for a while and don't want to shut it down and then reboot later. Without a screen saver, any confidential information on the screen can be seen by anyone nearby.

The screen saver is launched automatically after the computer has been inactive for a certain time, which you can set, as discussed shortly. The pattern or moving images are displayed until you click a mouse, press a key or tap a touch screen, etc. The computer then returns to its original state with the same apps and files open.

As discussed shortly, there is an option to display the Lock screen on returning from the screen saver. This requires a password to be entered before anyone can access your files.

Setting Up a Screen Saver

From the bottom of the Lock screen settings window shown below, select **Screen saver settings**.

Screen saver settings

The **Screen Saver Settings** window opens, as shown on the next page.

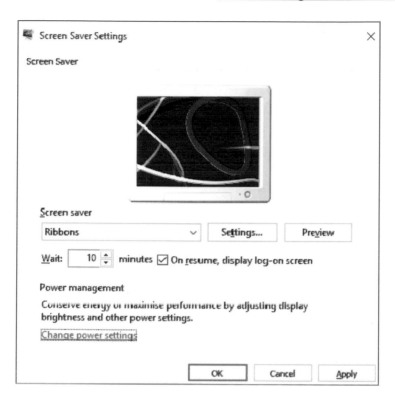

Under **Screen saver** above you can choose from a number of screen patterns such as the **Ribbons** example shown at the top. Or select **Photos** and **Settings** to set up a slide show of your own photos as a screen saver.

Wait shown above is used to set the number of minutes of computer inactivity before the screen saver is launched.

Tick the box next to **On resume,...** shown above to display the Lock screen and require a password to be entered. When the correct password is entered the computer will display the apps and files you were previously working on.

Sleep Mode

At the bottom of the **Lock screen** section of **PERSONALISATION** shown on pages 77 and 78, there is a link called **Screen timeout settings**. This opens the window shown below, which has settings for the power saving options **Screen** and **Sleep**. These are both standby states for when you are not using the computer for a while but don't want to shut down and reboot. **Screen** simply switches the screen off until you press a key, tap the screen, etc.

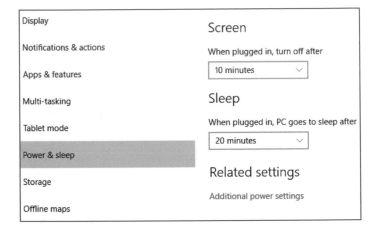

If you're using a battery powered machine, you can have different time settings depending on whether the device is running on battery power or plugged into the mains.

Sleep is a low power state which shuts much of the computer down but keeps any work you are doing in the RAM or memory. The computer is "woken" by pressing the power button or activating the mouse or keyboard. The computer then returns to its previous state with the same apps and files open. **Sleep** can also be selected from the **Power** option on the Start Menu, as shown on page 41.

Displaying the Lock Screen on Waking Up

If you select **Additional power settings** as shown on the lower right of the screenshot on the previous page, you are taken to the Windows Control Panel. Select **Require a password on wake-up** from the left-hand side to display the screen shown in part below.

Now select **Change settings that are currently unavailable** shown above. This allows you to switch on **Require a password**, (i.e. using the Lock screen), when waking up.

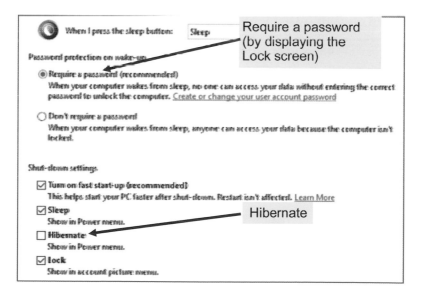

Hibernate

The **Hibernate** option automatically saves any open files to disc and then shuts down the computer.

Tick the box shown next to **Hibernate** at the bottom of page 83 to add **Hibernate** to the **Power** menu in the Start Menu as shown on the right and at the top of page 41.

Themes

If you select **Themes** then **Theme settings** shown under **PERSONALISATION** shown on the next page, you are given a choice of ready-made screen designs including different desktop backgrounds, colours and sounds. You can also save your own themes under **My Themes** shown below, based on your own photos or designs.

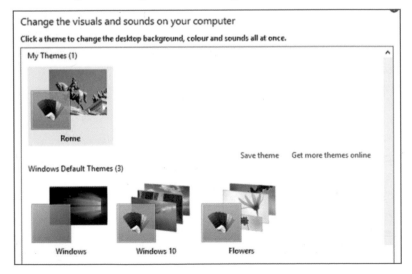

Customising the Start Menu

Start on the **PERSONALISATION screen** shown below allows you to decide what apps appear on the Start Menu. As shown below, the settings **Show most used apps** and **Show recently added apps** are both switched **On** by default.

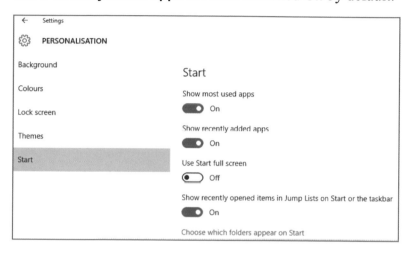

As shown above, you could also set the Start tiled area to occupy the whole screen by switching **Use Start full screen** to **On**. The last switch shown above **Show recently opened items in Jump lists on Start or the taskbar** displays the latest apps and folders you've been using on pop-up lists.

At the bottom of the above screenshot, tap the link **Choose which folders appear on Start**. As shown on the right and at the top of pages 38 and 84, **File Explorer** and **Settings** appear on Start by default.

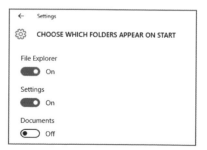

Key Points: Personalising Windows 10

- A choice of Windows pictures is available to use as the Desktop background. Or you can use your own pictures individually or as a slideshow.

- Dominant colours from your chosen background are incorporated into the Start Menu and Taskbar, etc.

- The Lock screen waits for a password to be entered when the computer starts up. Status updates from apps can be set to appear on the Lock screen.

- The Lock screen can be personalised with your own background picture or with a slideshow.

- A *screen saver* displays constantly changing patterns and images after a computer is inactive for a set time.

- The screen saver is *not a power saving mode*, since the computer is constantly working on the display.

- *Sleep mode* is a *low power consumption mode*, entered after a set period of inactivity. The *hibernate* option saves all the files currently open before shutting down a computer.

- You return a computer from a screen saver or "wake" it from sleep mode by pressing a key, etc., or tapping the screen. Before returning the computer to its previous working state, you can set the Lock screen to appear. A password is then required to proceed.

- The Start Menu can be customised to show the most used apps, recently added apps and to select which folders are to appear.

Ease of Access

Introduction

Windows 10 has a number of features to make a computer easier to use and to help with problems such as impaired vision or hearing, etc. These features include:

The Narrator

This reads aloud the text on the screen including the title bars and text in Windows as well as documents.

The Magnifier

This makes the screen easier to read by enlarging the entire screen area or just selected parts.

High Contrast

Text and backgrounds can be displayed in a choice of themes which use different colours.

Closed Captioning

Words spoken on TV or video displayed as text on the screen — like *sub-titles* but with additional information.

The On-Screen Keyboard

This is intended for anyone who finds the normal physical keyboard difficult to use.

Speech Recognition

Controlling the computer and inputting data by speaking.

The Narrator

Open the Start Menu by clicking or tapping the Start button shown on the right. Then select **Settings** from
the Start Menu and then select **Ease of Access** from the main **SETTINGS** window which opens. Alternatively click or tap the **New notifications** icon shown on page 68 and select **All settings** then **Ease of Access**.

Ease of Access
Narrator, magnifier,
high contrast

The **EASE OF ACCESS** screen opens as shown below.

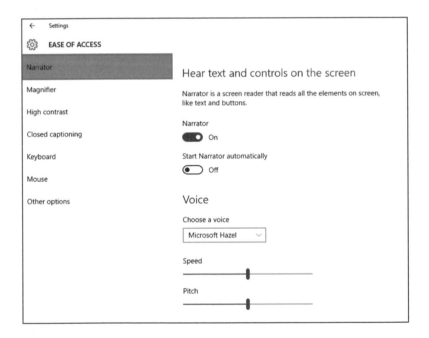

With the **Narrator** switched on as shown above, the chosen voice speaks aloud every key that you press. It also reads out the titles on windows and the names of new apps when you switch to them. There are three voices to choose from.

Reading Out Aloud Using Adobe Reader

Many documents which you can download from the Internet have been created in the PDF format. This file format is also an option when you save documents in apps such as Microsoft Word or Microsoft Publisher. Adobe Reader is the standard app for reading PDF files. This can be installed free from the Adobe Web site, **adobe.com**.

Open the required PDF document in Adobe Reader. Now select **View**, **Read Out Loud** and **Activate Read Out Loud**. Adobe Reader then reads aloud the paragraphs you select.

To read more of a document, select **Read Out Loud** again and select **Read This Page Only** or **Read to End of Document**. These options are no longer greyed out as they are when **Activate Read Out Loud** is first selected, as shown above. There is also an option to **Deactivate Read Out Loud**.

The Magnifier

Select **Magnifier** from the list shown on page 88, then switch **Magnifier On** as shown below.

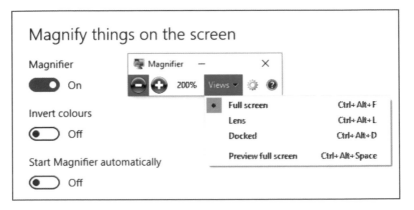

The **Magnifier** window opens, perhaps initially set at 200% but this can be changed using the plus and minus buttons shown above. If you tap or click the arrow next to **Views**, shown above, you can choose whether to enlarge the **Full screen** or just the **Lens**. The **Lens** is a small rectangle which can be dragged around the screen with a finger or mouse, enlarging different areas. The example below uses the **Lens** view at 200% magnification.

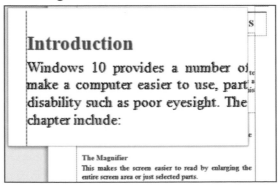

In **Docked** view a horizontal strip across the top of the screen is enlarged. The strip can be scrolled to display the whole document in large text, as a succession of strips.

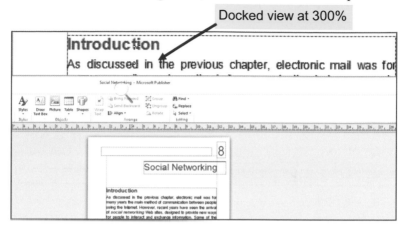

Docked view at 300%

After a short time the small Magnifier settings window shown below changes to a magnifying glass icon, as shown on the right. This icon can be tapped or clicked to make the Magnifier settings window reappear on the screen as shown below.

Tap or click the cross at the top right of the Magnifier settings window shown above to switch off the Magnifier.

High Contrast

This feature offers four different **High Contrast** colour schemes designed to make the screen easier to read.

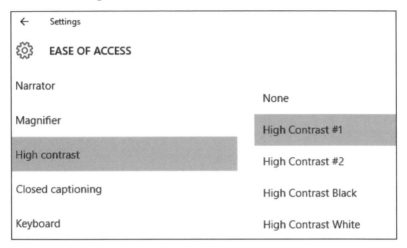

The Start Menu shown on the left below is displayed in the **High Contrast #1** format while **High Contrast White** is used for the example on the right below.

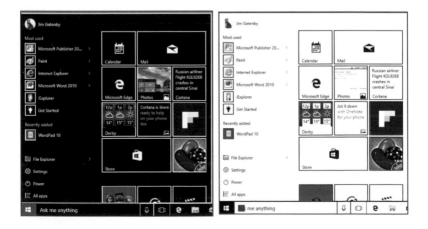

Selecting a High Contrast Screen

Select **Ease of Access** as described on page 88 and then select **High contrast**. After choosing a colour scheme from the four shown on page 92 select **Apply**. To return to the default Windows colour scheme select **None** as shown at the top right on page 92.

Closed Captioning

This option, shown under **EASE OF ACCESS** on page 92, allows you to display spoken words as text on the screen while watching a video or TV show. While the video is playing, right-click or hold over the screen to display a menu bar at the bottom. If closed captions are available, a **CC** icon should appear, as shown on the right and below right.

A *closed caption* is similar to a *sub-title*. Both display spoken words as text on the screen, but the closed caption may also include other information such as "door closes" or "owl hoots".

The On-Screen Keyboard

This is a special virtual keyboard in Windows 10, used on desktop and laptop computers as an alternative to the physical keyboard. It's not the same as the on-screen keyboard used as standard on tablets and smartphones.

The on-screen keyboard in Windows 10 is operated by pointing and clicking the keys on the screen with a mouse. Open **EASE OF ACCESS** as discussed on page 88, select **Keyboard** and switch **On-Screen Keyboard On**, as shown below. This opens the On-Screen Keyboard, as shown on the next page.

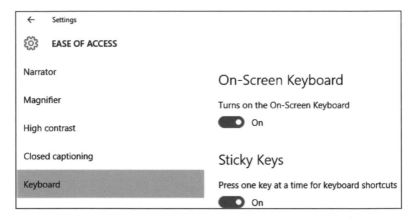

Keyboard shortcuts are combinations of key presses which perform many useful functions as an alternative to clicking with a mouse. For example, holding down the **Windows Key** and simultaneously pressing **A** opens the **ACTION CENTRE** discussed on page 68. Switching on **Sticky Keys** above allows you to use keyboard shortcuts by pressing only one key at a time on the On-Screen Keyboard. Many useful keyboard shortcuts are listed on page 96.

The On-Screen Keyboard is shown below, open on the screen in Microsoft Publisher.

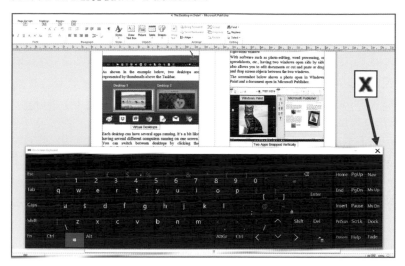

Unlike some on-screen keyboards on tablets, etc., the On-Screen Keyboard launched from Ease of Access, has a full range of keys including the Windows Logo key shown on the right and below, used in a lot of useful keyboard shortcuts.

If you have a touchscreen device, you may still find it useful to launch this On-Screen Keyboard from Ease of Access. This can also be operated with touch gestures.

You can move the On-Screen Keyboard window around the screen by dragging in the title bar. To close the On-Screen Keyboard, tap the cross at the top right-hand corner of the keyboard window shown above.

Keyboard Shortcuts

These are combinations of two or more key presses used to carry out actions which might otherwise be done by pointing and clicking with a mouse. A typical method is to hold down one key and then simultaneously press a second key. Or hold down two keys and press a third.

As discussed earlier, if you're using the On-Screen Keyboard launched from the Ease of Access Centre, with Sticky Keys On, the keyboard shortcuts can be entered by clicking the keys *one at a time* with a mouse.

In the examples below, the Windows Logo Key is denoted by its usual icon, as shown on the right.

⊞	Open or close the Start Menu
⊞ + A	Open the Action Centre
⊞ + S	Open Cortana Search
⊞ + C	Open Cortana Listening
⊞ + Tab	Open Task View
⊞ + D	Display/hide the Desktop
⊞ + E	Open File Explorer

⊞ + I	Open Settings
⊞ + L	Lock PC, open Lock Screen
⊞ +Ctrl+D	Add a virtual desktop
⊞ +T	Cycle through apps on the Taskbar
⊞ +U	Open the Ease of Access Centre
⊞ +X	Open the Quick Link Menu
⊞ +Enter	Open/close Narrator
Ctrl+C	Copy the selected item or text
Ctrl+V	Paste the selected item or text
Ctrl+X	Cut the selected item or text
Alt+Tab	Switch between open apps
Ctrl+P	Print document
Ctrl+Z	Undo an action

Speech Recognition

This feature allows you to control the computer entirely by spoken commands. Speakers and a microphone are normally built into laptops and tablets, etc., but you may need to buy them separately for a desktop machine.

Tasks such as starting programs, opening menus, dictating text and sending e-mails can be achieved without using touch gestures, or a mouse or keyboard.

From the **SETTINGS** screen shown on page 69, select the icon shown on the right then select **Speech** and **Get started**. You are then given a piece of text to read, as shown below.

Time & language
Speech, region, date

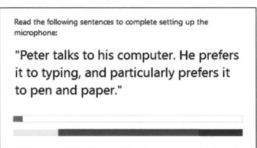

Read the following sentences to complete setting up the microphone:

"Peter talks to his computer. He prefers it to typing, and particularly prefers it to pen and paper."

All being well you should see the message shown below.

Your microphone is now set up.

The microphone is ready to use with this computer. Click Finish to complete the wizard.

To dictate some text, open an app such as Word and then, to open Speech Recognition, right-click or hold over the Start button at the bottom left of the screen. Then select **Control Panel** from the Quick Link Menu which appears followed by **Ease of Access** and **Start speech recognition**.

The microphone window appears as shown below, showing **Listening**, ready for you to speak some text.

To learn more, from the Control Panel select **Ease of Access** and **Speech Recognition** and then **Take Speech Tutorial** to learn about the speech commands for controlling the computer, dictation and editing documents.

Train your computer to understand you better shown above asks you to read a succession of sentences. This helps the computer to understand your voice and improve the accuracy of your dictation.

If the computer can't understand what you've said, "**What was that?**" is displayed in place of **Listening** shown above.

Tap the microphone icon shown at the top above to switch alternately between **Listening** and **Off**.

Key Points: Ease of Access

- The *Narrator* reads aloud the text on the screen, including keys pressed and titles of windows.

- The *Adobe Reader* app can read out aloud extracts or whole documents in the PDF file format.

- The *Magnifier* enlarges the text in full screen mode, or in a moveable Lens area or in a scrollable strip.

- *High Contrast* presents a choice of strong colour schemes designed to make the screen easy to read.

- *Closed Captioning* adds sub-titles and other information to TV programs and videos.

- *Keyboard shortcuts* allow many mouse or touch operations to be performed quickly and easily by pressing two or three keys simultaneously.

- The *On-Screen Keyboard* in the Ease of Access Centre is used with a mouse or touch. This allows keyboard shortcuts to be entered one key at a time.

- *Speech Recognition* requires a suitable microphone to be set up and tested and the computer should be trained to understand your speech.

- Speech Recognition can be used to control a computer using *voice commands* such as to open and close apps, select options from menus and *dictate* and edit text.

Cortana

Introduction

Cortana is a digital personal assistant, designed to carry out the functions of a human PA. It's named after a female character in Microsoft's Halo video game. At the time of writing it's planned to have versions of Cortana for all of the main computer, tablet and smartphone platforms including Google's Android and Apple's iOS, as well as Microsoft Windows.

Searching for different types of information from various sources is one of Cortana's main functions. Information may be obtained from your device's own internal storage, from the Internet including the "Clouds" and from your local area. Uses of Cortana include:

- *Spoken* or *typed* search queries on any subject.
- *Spoken commands* to do something, like opening an app such as Paint.
- Keeping a *Notebook* of your interests, contacts, local information, weather, traffic news and sports.
- Setting up spoken *reminders* to do something at a certain time.
- Asking Cortana to tell you a *joke*.
- *Dictating* and sending *e-mails* using only spoken commands from start to finish.

Launching Cortana

The Cortana search bar is placed at the bottom left-hand corner of the screen, displaying the words **Ask me anything**. Click or tap anywhere in the search bar to display the Cortana Home panel shown below.

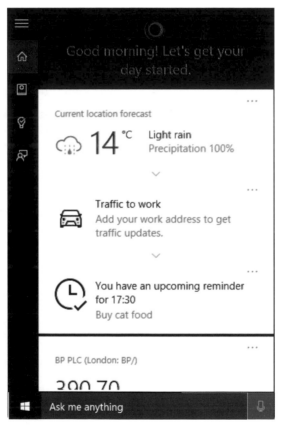

As shown above, the Home panel in Cortana shows the weather in your current *location*. You can also receive traffic information if you enter, say, your work address. In this example there is also a notification to **Buy cat food**.

The Home panel shown on the previous page can also be opened by clicking or tapping **Cortana** on the All apps menu or selecting the Cortana tile on the Start Menu.

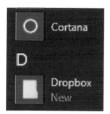

Clicking or tapping the 3-bar menu icon shown on the right and at the top left of the Home panel shown on the previous page opens the main **CORTANA** menu shown below on the left.

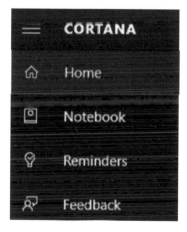
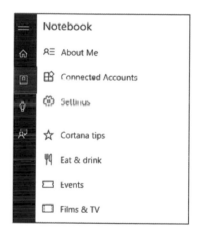

As shown in the extract on the right above, the **Notebook** contains a great deal of information about you and your preferences. As discussed later, the **Notebook** also allows you to switch several important settings On and Off.

Reminders are discussed in detail shortly. **Feedback** allows you to tell Microsoft what you think of Cortana.

Searching for Information

Cortana works with the Bing search engine to find information on any subject.

Typing the Keywords

You can enter your search criteria by typing the keywords into the search bar at the bottom left of the screen, as shown below, replacing the words **Ask me anything**.

Enter the keywords as shown below and press the Enter or Return key. The search is carried out by Bing and the first few results are shown below.

The Voice Search

Click or tap the microphone icon shown on the right and on page 104. The word **Listening** is then displayed as shown below.

Now speak the key words and all being well the words should be displayed in the search bar as shown on page 104. Speaking the words "green woodpecker" produced exactly the same search results as the search when the keywords were typed, as shown at the bottom of page 104.

However, sometimes a spoken query results in a *spoken answer*, as well as a screen display. For example, try saying "Weather in Barcelona" and Cortana *says aloud* "Right now it's 19 and mostly sunny in Barcelona". A link at the bottom of the screen allows you to see the full list of Bing search results similar to the list at the bottom of page 104.

The Cortana Home panel also gives examples of the sort of questions you can ask, as shown below.

Settings

Although many searches still produce the more traditional Bing list of search results, rather than spoken answers, it's a lot quicker to speak your questions rather than typing them. As discussed shortly, using Cortana's speech recognition is also a very quick way to send an e-mail without touching either a physical or on-screen keyboard.

To get the most out of Cortana's speech recognition you may need to do some setting up. With a desktop computer you may need to obtain a separate microphone. You will also need to select **Settings** in the Cortana **Notebook** as discussed on page 103. This opens the **Settings** window shown on the next page.

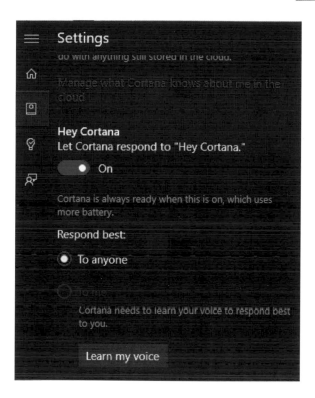

Training Cortana

If you switch **Hey Cortana** On as shown above, whenever you say "Hey Cortana", Cortana starts listening. Although, as stated above, this option does use more battery.

If you tap **Learn my voice** shown above, Cortana gives you six sentences to speak. This should help you to use speech recognition for a wide range of activities. A full list of these can be viewed after entering "What can I say to Cortana" into the Cortana search bar.

b bing   What can I say to cortana?

Tracking Flights

Tap or click the microphone to switch listening then speak the flight number.

Cortana then says "Here's what I've found" and the following information is displayed in the Home panel.

Maths

For example, speak the following multiplication sum.

Cortana speaks the answer, saying "That makes one thousand and seventy three" and also displays the answer on the calculator screen as shown below.

Setting an Alarm

From the All apps menu on the Start Menu select, **Alarms & Clock** and make sure **Alarm** is switched **On**. When Cortana is **Listening** say "wake me at twelve fifteen pm" or "wake me in half an hour" and the alarm will ring while displaying the **Snooze** and **Dismiss** buttons as shown below.

Sports Results

You might ask for the latest result from your favourite football team, for example.

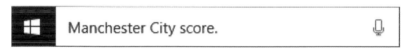

This produced a spoken answer from Cortana as well as the result displayed on the Cortana Home panel shown below.

Some useful search results are displayed including the **Windows Phone** link shown below.

What can I say to Cortana? - Windows Phone
www.windowsphone.com/en-US/how-to/wp8/cortana/what-can-i-say-to... ▾
Here are some ideas for what you can say to Cortana, and how she can help out.

Clicking or tapping the above link displays a comprehensive list of spoken commands and questions you can put to Cortana.

Chatting to Cortana

A few examples of spoken input for you to practise are shown below. First click or tap the microphone icon or say "Hey Cortana" so that the search bar displays **Listening** as shown on page 105.

Now say the following to Cortana or perhaps make up some more of your own.

- How are you today?
- How old are you?
- Where are you from?
- Where do you live?
- Tell me a joke.
- Toss a coin.
- Local restaurants.
- Roll a die.

Spoken Commands

You can give Cortana spoken commands, such as to launch an app. For example, to open the Microsoft Edge Web browser, make sure Cortana is **Listening** as discussed on page 105 and then say "Open Microsoft Edge".

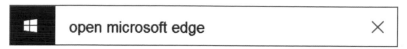

The following appears on the Cortana Home panel.

Microsoft Edge then opens on the screen ready for you to start browsing. You can use spoken commands to launch other apps and settings. Listed below are some you might try:

Paint	OneNote	Settings	Control Panel
Calendar	Calculator	OneDrive	File Explorer

Make sure Cortana is **Listening** and say, for example, "Open Paint".

Setting a Reminder

Click or tap in the Cortana bar at the bottom left of the screen. Then select the Reminders icon shown on the left, on the Cortana Home panel which pops up as shown below.

Next select the plus sign at the bottom of the Cortana Home panel as shown below, to set up a new reminder.

The dialogue box shown at the top of the next page then appears, ready for you to enter the details of the reminder. Enter the reminder itself replacing the words **Remember to**.... You can set a reminder to be displayed when you next contact someone by e-mail etc., visit a certain place or at a particular time. (*Location services* allow a mobile computer such as a laptop, tablet or smartphone, etc., to pinpoint your location using GPS satellite navigation.)

The reminders are displayed when needed, in the following screen locations:

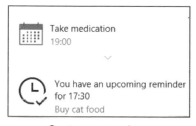

Cortana panel

Calendar

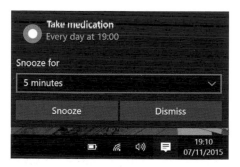

Notification Area

Calendar tile on Start Menu

Sending a Voice-only Email

Cortana allows you to send an email using only voice commands and dictation. This is obviously very useful if you're on the move or you find typing difficult. Say "Hey Cortana" to make sure she is listening then say "Send email". Your spoken words appear in the search bar.

Cortana then asks who you are sending your email to.

You can then speak the name of your recipient. (Or if you wish you could tap or click the + shown above and choose the recipient(s) from your contacts list which appears).

In this example, using speech only, the name "Jill" was spoken. As there were two contacts including "Jill", Cortana says "Which Jill?" and the message shown at the top of the next page appeared.

After speaking the name of your intended recipient you are asked to enter a subject and then speak the message.

After you say "Send", the message is sent and Cortana confirms it as shown below.

Key Points: Cortana

- Cortana is a *virtual personal assistant*, designed to work with most types of computer.

- A wide range of information is available from Cortana such as local amenities, weather, flight and traffic, sports results and answers to maths questions.

- You can search for information or give commands using *voice recognition* or keyboard input.

- Voice input requires Cortana to be *listening,* enabled by clicking or tapping a microphone icon.

- Listening is also started by saying "Hey Cortana". This must be switched on in the Notebook Settings.

- Cortana gives spoken answers to some queries or uses the Bing search engine to produce a list of Web sites displayed in the Microsoft Edge browser.

- To help Cortana understand you, open **Learn my voice** in Settings and practise reading the sentences provided.

- Spoken commands can *open applications* or set an *alarm*, such as "wake me in half an hour".

- You can set *reminders* to appear in the Cortana panel, in the Notifications area and on the Calendar, at certain times, when you contact someone or visit a place.

- Emails can be created, dictated and sent using only spoken commands from start to finish.

Microsoft Edge

Introduction

Microsoft Edge is a new *Web browser* introduced with Windows 10. A Web browser is an app used to navigate the vast number of pages of information stored on millions of Internet computers around the world. Microsoft Edge is the successor to Internet Explorer, which has been supplied with the Microsoft Windows operating system for many years. Internet Explorer continues to be very popular and is still available within Windows 10, as discussed on page 58.

Popular rival Web browsers include Google Chrome and Mozilla Firefox. Microsoft was forced to offer a choice of Web browsers included within Microsoft Windows after a legal battle with the EEC. This applied to Windows 7 and 8/8.1 but the legal requirement has now expired and Windows no longer offers a choice of browser other than Microsoft Edge and Internet Explorer.

Microsoft Edge has a completely redesigned user interface and some useful new features, such as built-in tools which allow you to draw and make notes on a Web page, before sending a copy to a friend. You can display and print Web pages in *Reading View*, stripping away any non-essential notices and adverts, etc., and showing only the core text of the document. Perhaps most significantly, tests have also shown that Microsoft Edge is faster at navigating Web pages than other Web browsers.

Functions of Microsoft Edge

- To display relevant Web pages after you enter keywords into a *search engine* (a program) such as Bing or Google.

- To work with Cortana to display Web pages resulting from searches using *voice input* as well as keyboard entry of the search keywords.

- To open Web sites after their unique addresses are typed into the Address Bar in the browser.

- To carry out a search after entering the keywords into the Address Bar in Microsoft Edge.

- To navigate between different Web pages using *hyperlinks*, i.e. highlighted words on the Web pages which can be clicked or tapped.

- To use *tabs* at the top of each Web page to move between pages.

- Use *forward* and *back* buttons to move between Web pages.

- To save *bookmarks* i.e. links allowing you to return to *favourite* or recently visited Web sites.

- To list the Web sites you've visited in the *History* feature.

- To allow the user to pin a Web site to the Start Menu in the form of a *tile*.

Launching Microsoft Edge

There are several ways to launch Microsoft Edge. You can tap or click its icon on the Taskbar at the bottom of the screen, as shown in the centre below.

Or select its tile on the Start Menu, as shown on the right. There is also an icon for Microsoft Edge on the All apps section of the Start Menu, as shown below.

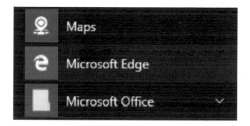

Or you can launch Edge by saying "Hey Cortana" and then saying "Open Microsoft Edge".

Searching Using Microsoft Edge

As discussed on page 118 and in the previous chapter, there are several ways to start a search for information. These include clicking or tapping the Microsoft Edge icon as discussed on page 119. This opens Edge with the search bar ready for you to enter the keywords of your choice, as shown in the example below:

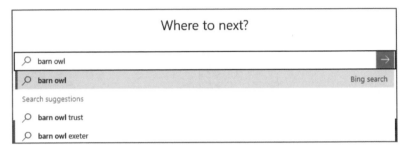

In the above example, when you type the keywords **barn owl**, Edge responds with some suggestions underneath your entry, such as **barn owl trust** shown above. Click or tap the magnifying glass icon next to the keywords you've entered or next to one of the suggestions.

As shown below, the *Bing search engine* produces a list of over a million results for the barn owl search.

Although there are many thousands of search results, they may not all be relevant. For example, the search will probably list several pubs known as the Barn Owl. Fortunately, the Web browser places the most relevant results at the top of the list.

The blue text in a search result as shown at the bottom of page 120 is a *hyperlink* to a Web page. Click or tap the blue link to open the Web page, such as **The Barn Owl Trust page** shown below.

Searching Using Cortana

The same result could be obtained by typing or speaking the keywords into the Cortana bar at the bottom left of the screen as shown below and discussed in Chapter 7.

Changing the Category to be Searched

As shown below and at the bottom of page 120, you can change the category of the information in which Bing is searching.

As shown above, by default the Bing search engine searches the entire **Web**. However, you can focus the search on particular categories such as **Images**, **Videos**, **Maps**, etc. If you select **Images** shown above, the following search results are displayed, where each image is a link to a larger picture.

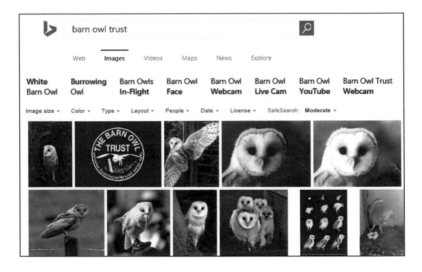

Similarly selecting the other headings shown above to the right of **Images** allows you to display links which open **Videos**, **Maps** and **News** items relating to the Barn Owl Trust.

Searching Using Google

Google is probably the most well-known search engine and can be used as an alternative to Bing. Google is available as an app in the Store and can be located and installed as described on pages 52 and 53.

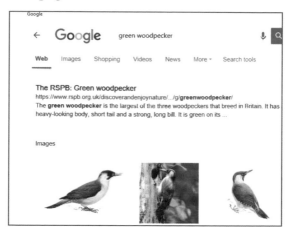

After launching from the Start Menu, All apps, or the Taskbar, Google can be used for searching using typed or spoken keywords in a similar way to Microsoft Edge.

Upper and Lower Case Letters in Keywords

barn owl trust yields the same results as **Barn Owl Trust**.

Inverted Commas

"red squirrel" will eliminate unwanted results, such as a page containing "a grey **squirrel** was eating **red** berries".

Narrowing a Search

Add extra keywords to search more accurately – e.g. **greater spotted woodpecker** rather than just **woodpecker**.

Entering a Web Address

Most companies, organisations and many individuals now have their own Web site, to publish news and information. Each Web site is identified on the Internet by a unique address or **URL** (*Uniform Resource Locator*). Many organisations include their address on their correspondence, in advertisements or on their vehicles, for example:

www.babanibooks.com

The Web address gives a very quick way to move directly to a particular Web site, without having to look through a list of search results, as with the keyword search. In Microsoft Edge enter the address under **Where to next?**

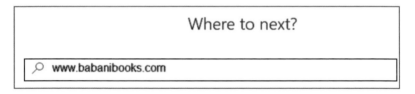

On pressing Enter or Return the Home page of the Web site quickly opens in Microsoft Edge, as shown below:

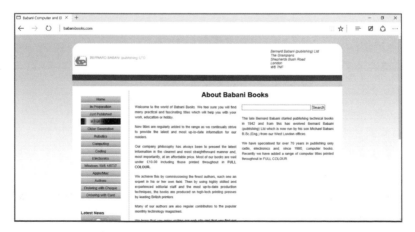

Navigating Around a Web Site

Within most Web pages there are numerous *links* or *hyperlinks*, usually in the form of text or images. If you pass a cursor over a link, the cursor changes to a hand. Tapping or clicking the link opens another page on the Web site or opens another Web site.

In the screen shot on the right, also shown near the bottom of page 124, each of the buttons **Home**, **In Preparation**, **Just Published**, etc., are links which lead to further Web pages.

The top left-hand corner of the Edge screen has several important controls, as shown below

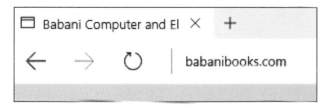

 Move **Back** or **Forward** through the recently visited pages.

 Refresh the Web page with the latest version.

Close the current Web page.

 Open a new *Tab*, as discussed on the next page.

Tabbed Browsing in Edge

Using a Single Tab

Tabs appear at the top of a Web page and show the names of the Web pages that have been opened. Depending on your settings, you may only be displaying one tab at a time.

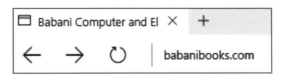

As you browse to open new Web pages, their title replaces the title of previous Web pages on the tab, as shown below.

In the example above, where a single tab is used to represent more than one Web page, you can cycle backwards and forwards through the Web pages using the arrow buttons shown above.

Opening New Tabs

However, if you click or tap the **+** sign as shown above, a **New tab** appears as shown below.

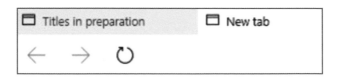

Now after doing a search, tap or click a link to open another Web page. The new Web page opens in the new tab, as shown below.

Alternatively, before opening another Web page from a link, right-click or hold and release over the link and select **Open in new tab** from the menu that appears, as shown below.

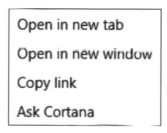

If you select **Open in new window**, as shown above, the Web page will be displayed in a tab on its own, as shown at the bottom of page 126.

If you choose to display several Web pages each with their own tabs across the screen as shown below, you can quickly move between pages by clicking or tapping the tab.

Click or tap the cross in the tab to close the Web page.

On the top right-hand corner of the Microsoft Edge screen are several more important tool icons as shown below.

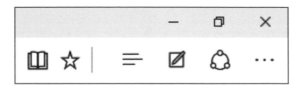

Reading View

With a Web page open in Microsoft Edge, click or tap the icon shown on the right and above. This opens Reading View, which strips away all of the peripheral text and images around a document. This makes it easier to read or print just the core of the main document as shown below.

Normal Web View

Reading View

Favourites

If you want to use a Web site regularly, you can add it to your list of Favourites after selecting the icon shown on the right and on page 128. Click or tap **Add** shown below to create a link to the Web site in the Microsoft Edge Hub as discussed shortly.

As described on page 58, to quickly revisit a Web site you can also place a *shortcut icon* on the Desktop.

The Favourites Bar

If you select the arrow in the **Create in** bar shown above, there is an option to add the Web site to the **Favourites Bar**, in addition to the **Favourites** list option. The Favorites Bar is a toolbar across the top of the Microsoft Edge screen, as shown below. This gives very quick access to Web sites.

To display the Favourites Bar, select the 3-dot **More actions** button in Edge as shown on the right and at the top of page 128. Then select **Settings** and make sure **Show the favourites bar** is switched **On**.

Reading list shown on the right and on page 129 works in a similar way to Favourites, to save documents for you to read later.

The Hub in Microsoft Edge

The Hub allows you to see your Favourites list, the Favourites Bar, the History list of the Web sites you've visited and any files you've downloaded from the Internet. Open the Hub by clicking or tapping its icon as shown on the right and at the top of page 128.

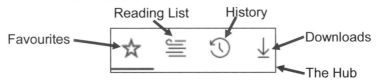

Viewing Your Favourites

The Hub opens with the list of **FAVOURITES** already displayed, as shown below. To open a Web page select its entry in the list. You can also open the **Favourites Bar** shown on page 129.

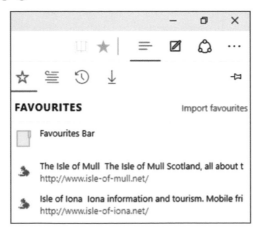

Viewing a Reading List

A Web site on the Reading list is opened by selecting the icon shown on the right and on page 130, then clicking or tapping the name on the list.

Viewing Your History

The History feature lists all of the Web sites you've visited in the last hour, during the current day and on previous days and weeks. Tap the icon shown on the right to open the **HISTORY** window shown below.

To revisit a Web page, tap the entry on the list, such as **M1 Traffic Map** shown above. Tap **Older** shown above to see Web sites you've visited in the last few months. Also shown above is an option to **Clear all history** and an icon to temporarily pin the **HISTORY** pane to the screen.

Viewing Your Downloads

This window shows all of the documents and programs you've downloaded from the Internet to your computer. Click or tap the icon shown on the right and below to open the **DOWNLOADS** window, also known as a pane.

Click or tap an item in the list to re-open a document or execute a downloaded program.

As shown above, there is a downloaded document in the Microsoft Word **.doc** format and several **.exe** files or programs used for installing and setting up software.

The icons for the three remaining features of Microsoft Edge not yet discussed are shown below, to the right of the icon for the Hub. Their functions are described below.

The Hub

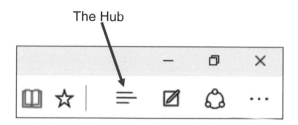

 Make a Web Note. After tapping or clicking this icon you can *annotate* a Web page with your own comments and freehand sketches, as shown on page 13. A set of icons for drawing and typing appears on the top left of the screen as shown below.

You can then send a copy of the page including your notes, etc.,to a friend, as discussed below.

 Send a link to open a Web page, using e-mail or social networking such as Twitter or Facebook. Or send the page to OneNote or your Reading List app for editing or reading later.

This icon at the top right of the Microsoft Edge window, also shown on page 133, opens the More Actions menu shown below.

The More Actions menu includes several useful options, including zooming in and out of a page and printing a Web page.

Pin to Start above places a *tile* on the Start Menu as discussed earlier in this book. This opens the Web page.

Maximising, Minimising and Closing Windows

The icons at the top right above appear on windows in general and have the following functions:

Minimise or reduce a window to an icon or thumbnail on the Taskbar.

Maximise the window to fill the screen.

Restore the window to its previous size.

Close the window.

Internet Security

A major type of Internet crime is *malware*, i.e. malicious software. Malware includes *viruses*, *worms* and *Trojan horses*. Viruses may be attached to e-mails or software and are designed to spread, cause damage to files and slow down computer systems and networks. Worms are similar to viruses but can spread on their own. The Trojan Horse poses as a legitimate piece of software but has an illegal purpose such as to give a hacker access to your computer. *Spyware* uses *phishing* to try to find out personal and financial information, such as your bank account details.

Sensible precautions include never answering e-mails appearing to be from your bank, asking you to confirm your account details. Real banks don't do this. You should also change your passwords regularly, as discussed below.

Changing Your Microsoft Password

Open the Start Menu and select **Settings** as shown on page 37. Then select **Accounts**, as shown on the right.

From the **Settings** menu select **Your account** followed by **Manage my Microsoft account** and then **Change password**. You will need your current password before entering and re-entering the new one. You can tell

Windows 10 to make you change your password every 72 days, as shown below.

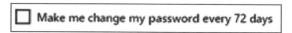

Windows 10 provides security software to combat these threats, as discussed on the next page.

Windows Defender

Windows Defender monitors your computer for viruses, spyware and malware and should always be switched On. You can also launch a manual scan using **Scan now** shown on the right of the screenshot on page 137.

Windows Firewall

The Windows Firewall is a barrier designed to stop hackers and worms from entering your computer.

Windows Update

Windows Update automatically downloads and installs the latest software upgrades from Microsoft, frequently intended to fix security problems. Many of the updates downloaded by Windows Update are new *virus definitions*. These allow anti-virus software such as Windows Defender to detect and eradicate the latest viruses.

You can check Windows Defender and Windows Update by selecting **All settings** in the Action Centre as discussed on page 68. Then select **Update & security** as shown on the right. You can make sure **Windows Defender** is **On** and check the status of **Windows Update** in the **UPDATE & SECURITY** window shown below.

Update & security
Windows Update,
recovery, backup

To review all of your security settings, right-click over the Start button and select **Control Panel**.

From the **Control Panel**, select **Review your computer's status** under **System and Security**.

Then select the downward pointing arrow to the right of **Security** to display all the settings. Make sure these are **On** or **OK**.

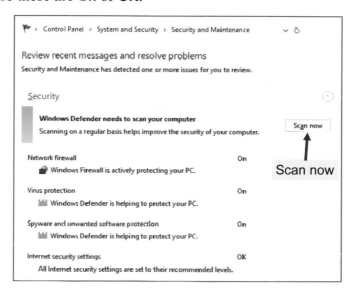

To switch settings **On** or **Off**, select **Change Security and Maintenance settings** on the left-hand side of the **Control Panel**.

Control Panel Home

Change Security and Maintenance settings

Third Party Security Software

Apart from the Windows 10 built-in security features, third -party Internet security, anti-virus and anti-malware software is available from companies such as Norton, Kaspersky, AVG and McAfee.

Key Points: Microsoft Edge

- Microsoft Edge is the new built-in *Web browser* for Windows 10. The previous browser, Internet Explorer, is still available in Windows 10.

- Edge works closely with Cortana and Bing to display Web pages after both *spoken* and *keyboard* searches.

- Edge can be launched from the All apps menu, the Taskbar, a tile on the Start Menu or by a Cortana.

- A *shortcut icon* to launch Microsoft Edge can be placed on the Windows 10 Desktop.

- The search bar in Microsoft Edge can be used to enter either *keywords* or *Web addresses*.

- You can move between Web pages using *forward* and *back* buttons, by creating *tabs* for new Web pages and by using *links* or *hyperlinks* on the Web pages.

- *Reading View* is used to make text-based Web pages easier to read by displaying only the main document.

- The *Favourites* feature and the *Reading List* allow you to quickly return to Web pages in the future.

- The *History* list provides links to reopen Web pages you've visited today and on recent days and weeks.

- The *Download* list shows links to documents and software you've copied from the Internet.

- The *Web Note* feature allows you add notes and sketches to a Web page then send it to someone else.

- Windows 10 Internet security features such as *Windows Firewall* and *Windows Defender* should be switched On, unless third party security software such as Norton, AVG or Kaspersky is installed instead.

Windows 10 Apps

Introduction

Whatever type of computer you use — laptop, desktop, tablet or smartphone — the choice of available apps or programs is critical. The range of Windows 10 apps covers productivity tools like word processors and spreadsheets, as well as games, maps, music, news, weather and entertainment. There are three main sources of apps for Windows 10:

- Apps built in to the Windows 10 operating system from new. These appear in the All apps menu and may also appear as tiles on the Start Menu.

- Apps available in the *Store*, downloaded to your device either free or to buy (usually for a few pounds). At the time of writing there are approximately 700,000 apps in the Store.

- Apps downloaded from Web sites or bought on a CD/DVD as part of a boxed package.

Apps on the All apps menu and on the Start Menu were discussed in Chapters 3 and 4. Downloading and installing an app from the Store was described in Chapter 4, together with creating icons and tiles for launching programs.

The Mail App

Electronic mail or e-mail has largely replaced the traditional letter as a method of sending information for business or social communication. Advantages of e-mail include:

- The message is delivered to its destination almost instantly. It is then immediately available to be read.
- The same message can be sent to many recipients, easily selected from an electronic address book.
- It is very simple for recipients to *reply* or *forward* the message to someone else.
- An e-mail can have files attached, such as text documents (like this chapter for example), spreadsheets, videos or photographs.
- Messages can easily be deleted or saved in an organised structure of folders, for future reference.
- E-mail can be used for long messages. Social networks like Twitter are limited to short messages.

Electronic mail might be used to communicate with long-lost relatives around the world, including the exchange of photographs. Documents, photographs and other files are "clipped" (metaphorically speaking) to the message and are known as *attachments*. The text in the body of the e-mail can be quite lengthy or it may simply be a covering note for any attachments. If you want a friend to see a particular Web site, you can embed a *link* to the Web site in the message. Your friend simply taps or clicks the link to launch the Web site.

The Mail app is built in to Windows 10 and can be launched using a tile on the Start Menu or icons on the All apps menu and on the Taskbar, as shown below.

Tile on Start Menu   All apps menu   Taskbar icon

Click or tap the tile or icon to open the Mail app as shown below. The left-hand panel shows the e-mails received in date order and the right-hand panel shows the currently selected message.

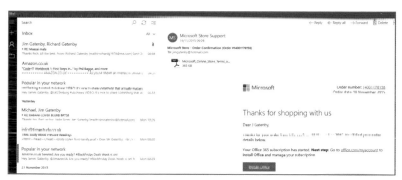

Creating an E-mail Account

You can either use your Microsoft account login or create a new e-mail account after clicking or tapping the **Expand** icon shown on the right. This appears in the top left-hand corner of the Mail screen. Then select **Accounts** as shown here on the lower right.

Now select **+Add account** from the accounts menu which appears at the top right of the screen and then choose Outlook.com to create a Microsoft account such as Outlook.com, Live.com, etc., as shown below.

The next window lets you sign in with an existing Microsoft account if you have one. Otherwise select **Create one**, as shown below.

No account? Create one

Then sign up to a new account as shown below. This new sign in can also be used to access other services such as the *Skype* Internet telephone service discussed shortly. Skype allows free calls worldwide between computers.

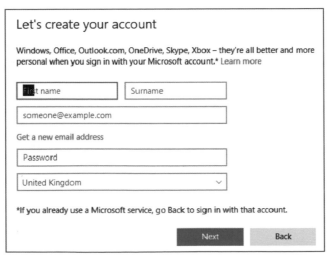

Creating an E-mail Message

Open the Mail App as described on page 141 and make sure the e-mail address you want to use is selected after selecting the **Expand** icon.

Now select **+New mail** shown above to open the window shown below, ready to type in the message.

Enter the name or names of the recipients and a **Title** on the line below, in this case **Maasai Mala**. Select **Cc** to add further people to receive the message (carbon copies) and **Bcc** to send *Blind carbon copies*. The **Bcc** recipients will receive the message unknown to the other recipients.

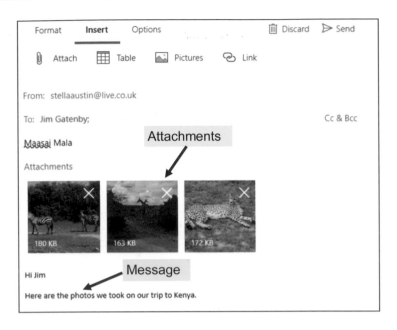

Inserting Photos, Pictures, Tables and Files

The **Insert** menu shown above allows you to **Attach** a file such as a photo, video or a document, etc., above the text of the message, as shown by the three thumbnail photos above. You can also insert a blank **Table** into which you can enter text and figures.

Selecting **Pictures** on the **Insert** toolbar shown above allows you to browse your hard drive, etc., for any photos and pictures to embed in the message in a large enough size to enable immediate viewing by the e-mail recipient. **Link** shown at the top of this page is used to insert a live Web address in the message.

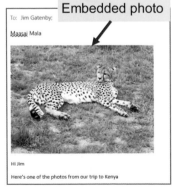

The recipients receive the first few lines of the e-mail in their **Inbox** as shown below.

Clicking or tapping inside this notification displays the message, shown below. The paperclip icon on the right shows that one or more files are attached.

Receiving an Attachment

Right-click or hold and release an attachment to **Save** the file or **Open** the file for viewing in its associated program.

Responding to an E-mail

As shown above, there are options to **Reply, Reply all** (to all recipients), **Forward** to someone else or **Delete** the message.

Skype

This is an Internet service which allows you to make free *voice* and *video* calls between computers. For example, you could see and speak to friends or relatives in New Zealand in real time without a call charge. All you need is computers at both locations connected to the Internet, equipped with microphones and speakers. To see each other in a video call you also need a webcam on each machine. The latest laptops, tablets and smartphones have all these accessories built in from new. If necessary, on desktop machines, these devices can be bought cheaply for a few pounds and fitted easily.

To download and install Skype, click or tap the **Get Skype** tile on the Start Menu, then follow the instructions on the screen.

During the setup process you are given the chance to test your microphone and Webcam. You can also take a Profile picture or browse your hard drive, etc., for a picture to use.

When the setup is complete, sign in with your Microsoft login name and password or create a new Skype account.

Launching Skype

An icon for Skype will appear on the All apps menu. This can used to launch Skype and start using it, as discussed on page 147. You can also add a tile for Skype on the Start Menu or an icon on the Taskbar, as discussed on pages 54 and 55, to launch Skype quickly.

Using Skype

Skype opens with a list of your contacts. Tap or click the required contact to see if they're **available**, as shown below.

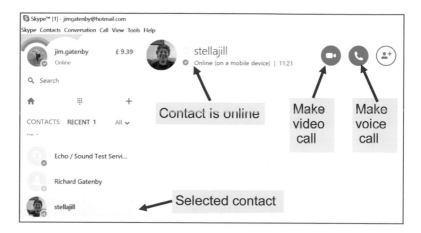

Making a Call

If the contact is online, click or tap the camera icon shown on the right to make a video call or select the phone icon to make a voice only call.
The contact's computer is then called as shown below.

Accepting a Call

After you tap or click to make a call, your contact will hear the dial tone and can tap or click their green phone or camera icon to accept the call, or the red icon to end it.

During a Call

When the other person accepts the call, their live picture or profile picture appears on your screen as shown below.

Icons to switch the video camera and the microphone on and off and to end the call are shown above. The icon shown on the right is used to allow other people to join in the conversation.

Calls to Mobiles and Landlines

If your contact is not online when you call, you can use Skype on your computer to call a mobile phone or landline. Unlike calls between two computers on the Internet, there is a charge for these calls. So you need a Skype account with a credit balance to make calls to a mobile phone or landline.

The Photos App

This apps lets you import, manage, edit and view photos on your laptop, desktop, tablet or smartphone. These may be photos taken using the Camera app on a Windows 10 device fitted with a Webcam. Alternatively photos may be imported from a separate storage medium such as an SD card from a camera or a flash drive/memory stick.

Importing photos is discussed shortly. Once imported and saved on your computer photos can be:

- Automatically *organised* into albums.
- *Enhanced* and *edited*.
- *Viewed* individually or as a *slide show*.
- Copied to *OneDrive* in the "clouds", to be viewed from anywhere on any computer.
- *Shared* with other people
- *Printed* on paper.

Using a Built-in Camera

If you have a built-in camera or a Web cam connected via a USB port you can take a photo using the **Camera** app, launched using its tile, shown on the right, on the Start Menu. Any

photo you take with the **Camera** app is saved in the **Camera Roll** in the **Pictures** section in **This PC**. This can be viewed, as shown on the right, as a *JPG file* in the **File Explorer** discussed in Chapter11.

Importing Images Using the Photos App

Many laptop and desktop machines have a slot which accepts a standard *SD card* from a digital camera. Tablets and smartphones usually have a *USB port* or a *microUSB port* to which you can connect an inexpensive *USB SD card reader*. (A special *OTG cable* is needed to connect a standard USB device to a microUSB port). You can also import photos from a *USB flash drive* (or *memory stick*), or a removable *hard drive* or *CD/DVD*.

With your SD card or external storage device connected to your computer, open the **Photos** app from its tile on the Start Menu.

Tap or click the **Import** icon shown on the right in the top right-hand corner of the **Photos** screen.

Then select with a tick the photos you wish to import from the SD card or storage device, as shown below.

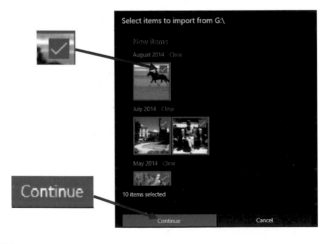

When you click or tap **Continue** shown at the bottom of the previous page, the photos are copied to your **Pictures** section in **This PC**.

Storage of Photos

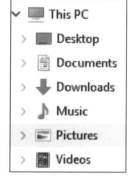

Photos taken with the built-in camera and also those imported using the **Photos** app are all stored in **Pictures** within **This PC** as shown on the right in the *File Explorer*. The File Explorer is discussed in Chapter 11.

Click or tap the **Photos** tile shown on the previous page. (If you right-click or hold and release the tile you can set it to display or switch off *live* thumbnails of your photos).

The Photos app opens displaying all your photos in the **COLLECTION** feature in date order. Click or tap any date to display a detailed list of all the dates.

Then click or tap a date to display all the photos taken on that date. **Albums** shown above are automatically created in **Photos** and you can also create your own. **Folders** above displays folders such as **Pictures** and **OneDrive** where photos are stored on your device.

Viewing and Editing a Photo

Click or tap a photo in the Collection, Albums or Folders to open the image on the full screen as shown below.

The toolbar at the top right of the screen is shown enlarged below.

The share icon is used to send a copy of the photo to someone else by e-mail or social network such as Facebook or Twitter. The **Edit** option above provides a comprehensive list of photo editing tools including **Rotate**, **Crop**, **Red eye**, **Straighten**, etc.

Selecting the 3-dot menu button shown on the right and on the toolbar above, opens the menu shown below on the right. **Open with** is used to open the photo in a different app, such as Paint. **Set as** allows you to use the photo as your Desktop background or as your Lock Screen or as the Photos tile on the Start Menu.

OneNote

OneNote provides a central location for all your scattered notes and information on scraps of paper, etc. OneNote is launched from its tile on the Start Menu shown on the right and includes the following features:

- You create a series of electronic *notebooks* divided into *sections*; each section can have several *pages*.

- Notes can be typed anywhere on the page and freely moved around in their own box or *container*.

- The page can contain text, pictures, tables, files, links to Web pages, etc.

- You can make and add audio and video recordings.

- You can make notes on a Web page using Microsoft Edge and *share* the page with OneNote.

- *Calculations* can be performed while you type.

- Pages are *saved automatically*.

- You can collaborate with colleagues using shared OneNote notebooks.

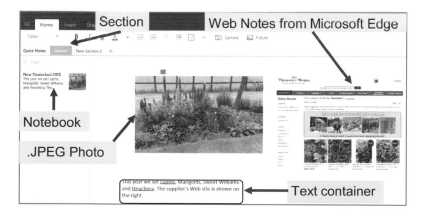

Further Apps

The previous pages have discussed some important apps in Windows 10, but there are many more. These two pages give brief outlines of some more very popular apps. Most of these are listed on the All apps menu and several also have tiles on the Start Menu.

UK and world news headlines and news in categories such as Finance, Technology, Sport and Entertainment. There is a live **News** tile on the Start Menu.

The is the weather forecast based on your location and also forecasts for other places found by name or postcode.

Breaking news, personal finance, company news and stock markets around the world with a live tile on the Start Menu.

View maps of your area, plan journeys, get traffic news. Search for places and local information around the world.

This is your contacts list where you can add people or edit their details.

If you have an Xbox games console you can stream games and play them on a PC computer in another room. There is an **Xbox** tile on the Start Menu.

Organise and play music already stored on your device. Buy new music from the Store. There is a **Groove Music** tile on the Start Menu.

Buy or rent films and TV programmes from the Store. Organise and play them on your device. There is a **Films & TV** tile on the Start Menu.

A tile on the Start Menu lets you download Fresh Paint from the Store. Fresh Paint lets you simulate sketching with a pencil, drawing with a pen or painting with oil or water colours. Activity packs with templates can be purchased.

Record events and set reminders which will pop up on the screen at the required time, as discussed in Chapter 7.

Key Points: Windows 10 Apps

- Apps may be *built into* Windows 10 from new, or *downloaded* from the Store or obtained separately.

- The Mail app can be used to send quite long messages with *attached* files such as photos, documents or videos. Photos may be embedded in the text.

- Skype allows *free* international phone calls including video between computers. A *charge* is made for calls to mobiles and landlines from your computer.

- The Photos app is used to view, store, organise and edit photos on a computer or smartphone.

- Photos may be taken using the *built-in camera* on your device or *imported* using the Photos app from media such as an SD camera card or a flash drive.

- Photos can be saved on the OneDrive Web site in the "clouds", making them accessible to you from *any computer* in any location with an Internet connection.

- OneNote is used to store all sorts of information from many different sources in a single location or *notebook* on your computer. Information includes notes, photos, videos and links to Web sites.

- Groove Music and Films & TV allow you to *buy* or *rent* music, films and TV programmes and organise and play them on your Windows 10 device.

- The Xbox app allows you to *stream* games from an Xbox console and play them on a desktop, laptop, etc.

- Latest information relating to your local area is provided by the Weather and Maps apps.

- The People app allows you to edit your contacts list.

Microsoft Office 365

Introduction

Office 365 is the latest version of Microsoft Office, the world's leading software used by businesses, educational institutions, students and home users for many years. It has been reported that there are over 1 billion users of Office worldwide and already over 2 million users of Office 365.

The main apps or programs making up Office 365 are:

- Word 2016 (word processor)
- Excel 2016 (spreadsheet)
- Publisher 2016 (desktop publishing)
- OneNote 2016 (digital notebook)
- PowerPoint 2016 (presentations)
- Access 2016 (database)
- Outlook 2016 (e-mail and calendar)

Overviews of most of the above apps are given in the rest of this chapter.

The Office suite has been a major factor in making Windows by far the most popular operating system in the world. As discussed shortly, Windows 10 has a tile on the Start Menu to enable users to easily obtain Office 365.

Office 365 Personal edition can be bought currently for £5.99 per month (or £59.99 per year). Office 365 works closely with the Microsoft Cloud Storage system OneDrive. 1TB (Terabyte), of free storage on OneDrive in the "clouds" is provided with Office 365. (1TB is 1000MB).

Universal Software

Office 365 is an example of *universal software* — it can be used on a wide range of devices — desktop, laptop, tablet and smartphone, running various operating systems such as Microsoft Windows 10, Apple iOS and Google Android.

A subscription to Office 365 Home edition (currently £79.99 per year) allows it to be used on 5 different devices. So you can continue working on documents using any computer, tablet, etc., wherever you happen to be.

Getting Office 365

To obtain Office 365, click or tap the **Get Office** tile, shown on the right, on the Windows 10 Start Menu. Then follow the instructions on the screen to download and install the software. You may need to scroll to see the tile. There is also an option to try the software free for a month.

When the installation of the software is complete, icons for each app or program appear on the All apps menu within the Start Menu. Click or tap the

Start button shown here on the upper right, in the bottom left-hand corner of the screen. Then select **All apps** as shown on the right.

The newly installed Office 365 apps, such as **Excel 2016**, appear separately on the All apps menu. Their position in the list is determined by alphabetical order, as shown in the small extract on the left below. Or you can select **Recently added** on the Start Menu to see all of the Office 365 apps just installed. You may need to click or tap **Expand** (which changes to **Collapse**) to see the whole list of Office 365 apps, shown on the right below.

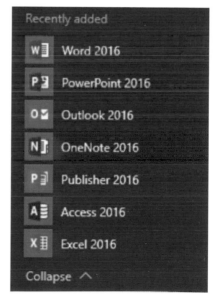

To reduce the **Recently added** list shown on the right, to its original size, select **Collapse**, as shown on the bottom right.

Accessing Your Favourite Apps in Office 365

To access frequently used apps such as Word 2016 and Excel 2016 you can create tiles on the Start Menu and icons on the Taskbar.

Creating a Start Menu Tile

To create a tile on the Start Menu for Word 2016, for example, right-click over its icon on the All apps menu as shown on the above right and select **Pin to Start** from the menu which opens as shown below.

Creating a Taskbar Icon

To create an icon for Publisher 2016, for example, from the right-hand menu shown above, select **Pin to taskbar** to create the Publisher 2016 icon shown on the right and on the Taskbar below.

Launching Office 365 Apps

In the examples which follow, each app such as Word 2016, etc., can be launched from the All apps menu, or alternatively from a Start Menu tile or an icon on the Taskbar, if you've created them as discussed above.

Word 2016

This is amongst the most popular software in the world, launched in 1983 and having many new versions up to the latest edition, Word 2016. Word can be used to produce any sort of a document from simple memos, letters, reports, CVs, legal documents, up to a full-size thesis or a book.

Text Formatting

Word 2016 contains many of the text formatting features previously found in dedicated desktop publishing software. These include text in different *fonts* or styles of lettering and effects such as italics, bold and underline together with bulleted or numbered lists.

Tables, photos, drawings and images from libraries of ready-made *clipart* can be inserted within the text.

The Tabbed Ribbon

As shown below, the *tabbed ribbon* is used to select the many tools, menus and features in Word 2016.

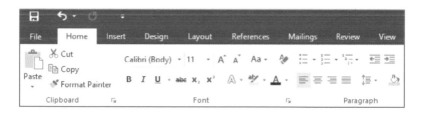

Similar tabbed ribbons are used in other apps in Office 365 such as Excel 2016 and Publisher 2016, etc. The **File** tab shown above has many options including starting a new document, opening a saved file, saving and printing documents or sharing with other people using e-mail, for example.

Publisher 2016

As mentioned earlier, Word 2016 has many of the features of a desktop publishing program. In fact I previously used Word for many of my books similar to this one. The main reason I changed to Publisher was because it was more suitable for commercial printing. Later software such as Word 2016 and Publisher 2016 allow you to save documents in the universal PDF format, compatible with commercial printers and widely used on the Internet.

Microsoft Publisher is especially good for the precise location and movement of text and pictures, with horizontal and vertical rulers to improve accuracy. It's therefore more suitable for the production of graphics-rich documents such as posters, banners, business cards, brochures and flyers, as well as books. Shown below are two pages from this book being edited in Publisher 2016.

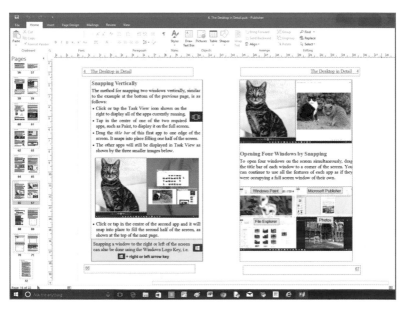

Excel 2016

Microsoft Excel has been the leading *spreadsheet* program for many years. Although designed to work mainly with numbers, it shares many features with Word and Publisher just discussed. Excel 2016 uses a tabbed ribbon like Word 2016 (shown on page 161) and Publisher 2016 and there are tools for formatting text in different fonts and colours.

The main use of Excel 2016 is for working with tables of figures, for tasks such as calculating total sales in a business, working out averages or estimating future trends. Built-in *functions* simplify these common calculations.

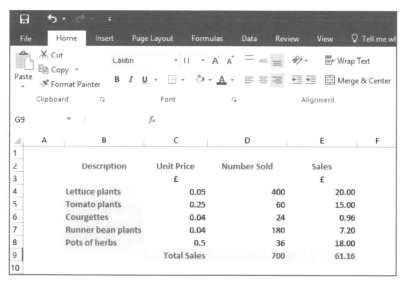

Replication makes it easy to enter a formula once then apply it, by dragging, to all of the rows or columns.

Excel 2016 makes it easy to present information in the form of graphs such as pie charts and column graphs.

PowerPoint 2016

PowerPoint 2016 is widely used for business presentations to large audiences but is also a very convenient tool for creating interesting family slide shows or to illustrate an informal talk to a club or group of friends. PowerPoint 2016 is used to:

- Create a series of digital "slides" consisting of separate pages of text, graphics and multi-media.

- You can add sound such as a commentary.

- Slides can be moved on automatically, changing after pre-set viewing times have elapsed.

- Alternatively slides can be changed using a mouse or touch.

- Many different templates and graphical designs and animations are available to polish the presentation.

- A PowerPoint presentation, as shown below, can be viewed on the Internet or sent across the world as a file attached to an e-mail.

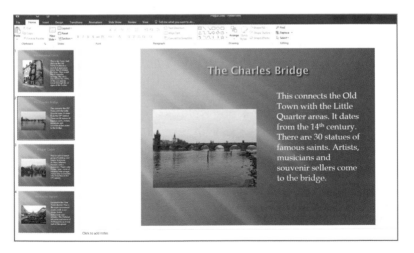

Access 2016

Microsoft Access 2016, shown below, is a *database* program. A database is a file consisting of a number of *records*, such as the names and addresses of employees in an organisation or students in a college. Each record consists of several *fields*, such as Name, Age, Address, etc.

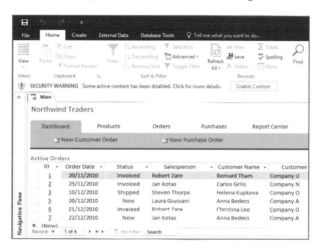

Advantages of a computerised database include the fact that records can easily be *updated* and *edited*, files can be *searched* to find a particular record and records can be rapidly *sorted* into *alphabetical* or *numerical order*.

OneNote 2016

Apart from the toolbar ribbon across the top of the screen, this is virtually the same as the edition of OneNote built into Windows 10 and outlined in Chapter 9.

Outlook 2016

Apart from the toolbar ribbon, this app is similar to the Mail app in Windows 10, discussed in Chapter 9.

Key Points: Microsoft Office 365

- Office 365 is the leading office productivity software used worldwide by organisations and individuals.

- Office 365 is *universal software*, i.e. used on all types of computers, tablets and smartphones running the Windows, iOS and Android operating systems.

- The **Get Office** tile on the Start Menu enables you to buy, download and install Office 365.

- All the Office 365 apps such as Word 2016 and Excel 2016 are listed separately on the All apps menu. You can also create *tiles* on the *Start Menu* and *icons* on the *Taskbar* to give quick access to each app.

- Word 2016 allows the creation of all sorts of documents such as letters, reports, memos, CVs, etc., with many Desktop Publishing features.

- Publisher 2016 is a Desktop Publishing app giving precise control over page layout and graphics, with support for *commercial printers*.

- Excel 2016 is the top spreadsheet for calculations on tables of figures and for producing graphs and charts.

- OneNote 2016 stores all types of text, pictures and multi-media information in *digital notebooks*.

- Access 2016 is a database used to create large files of *records* such as names and addresses. Records can be *searched*, *edited* and *sorted* into a particular order.

- PowerPoint 2016 is used to create *slideshow presentations* for both business and social audiences.

- Outlook 2016 is an e-mail program, with a calendar and other features and is similar to Windows 10 Mail.

Managing Files and Folders

Introduction

Everything we save on a computer is contained in a *file*. For example, a simple letter or report entered into Word 2016 would be saved as a file on your *internal storage* such as a hard disc drive, or an SSD (Solid State Drive). After selecting **File** and **Save As** in Word 2016 you enter a **File name**, such as **Latest news** shown below.

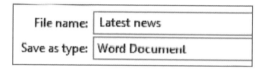

By default, this letter would be saved with **Word Document** as the file type as shown above. After selecting a *folder*, in this case **Correspondence**, in which to save the file, it is saved in the internal storage as shown below in the *File Explorer*, discussed in more detail shortly.

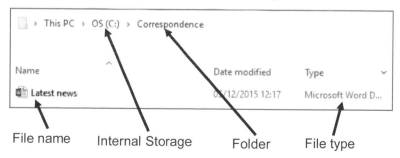

In this example, using a PC computer, the internal storage is a magnetic hard disc **OS(C:)**, shown above. In tablets and smartphones the internal storage is usually an SSD.

Filenames

When we save a document, a picture or a photograph, etc., we make up a *filename* to identify the file at a later date. The computer automatically adds a *filename extension*, such as **.docx** for a Microsoft Word 2016 document, as shown below.

Latest news.docx

Filename Extensions

Files are used to store all sorts of data, apart from text and numbers. There are files for photos, drawings, music, and video, etc. Apps themselves are stored as *executable files*. Each of the file types is identified by its own filename extension as shown in some common examples below.

.docx	Microsoft Word document
.doc	Microsoft Word 1997-2003 document
.pub	Microsoft Publisher file
.wma	Windows media audio file
.wmv	Windows media video file
.xls	Excel spreadsheet file
.jpg	Photographic file
.bmp	Bitmap format for graphics images
.pdf	Adobe Acrobat Document
.exe	Windows executable file (used for saving programs or apps)

So a photo might be saved as **ourcat.jpg**, a spreadsheet might be **accounts.xls** and a document might be **cv.pdf**.

The File Explorer

Previously known as the Windows Explorer, this is a *file manager* app. The File Explorer gives access to all of your files on your internal storage, in the clouds on the Internet, such as OneDrive or Dropbox, or on external plug-in devices such as flash drives and SD cards. Shown below is the **File Explorer**, with the **Quick access** feature open.

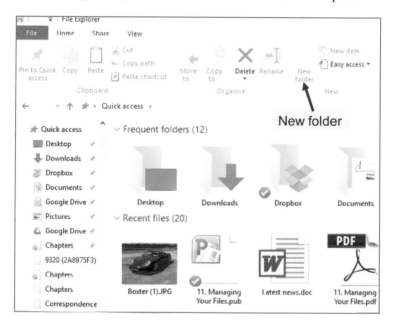

The **Quick access** feature shows in yellow the **Frequent folders** you've used. Folders are discussed shortly and are simply a collection of related files. You can create your own folders after selecting **New folder** shown above.

Recent files shows that I have been using a **.jpg** photo, this chapter in both Publisher **.pub** and **.pdf** formats and the letter **Latest news** in Word 2016 **.doc** format.

Launching the File Explorer

In Desktop view, an icon for the File Explorer appears on the Taskbar across the bottom of the screen.

The File Explorer can also be launched from the Start Menu after clicking or tapping the Start button in the bottom left corner of the screen.

The left-hand panel of the File Explorer lists the main storage areas on your device, as shown below. In this example, both Dropbox and OneDrive are cloud or Web storage areas. **KINGSTON (G:)** shown below is a flash drive plugged into a USB port on the computer.

Click or tap any of the storage areas shown above to view the folders and files within.

For example, selecting **This PC** shown on the previous page and below displays the local folders on the computer, tablet or smartphone and any external devices connected.

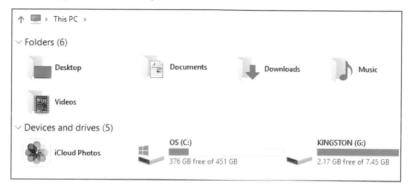

Subfolders can be created within folders after selecting the main host folder then selecting **New folder** shown below and entering the name of the subfolder.

The ribbon across the top of the File Explorer has options to change the **View** of the files and folders, such as **Extra large icons**, **Small icons**, a **List** and **Details** of files.

Opening a Folder and Managing Files

In the File Explorer double-click the folder or hold and release then tap **Open**. Then right-click or tap and hold a filename to display a menu including the options below.

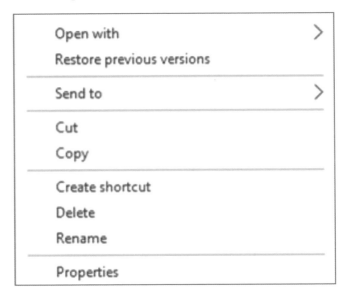

As shown above there are options to **Send** a file to various destinations such as a **Desktop shortcut** or an e-mail contact. **Cut** or **Copy** can be used together with **Paste** off the File Explorer ribbon shown on page 171, to move or copy a file to another folder. Files can also be copied by *dragging and dropping* as discussed on pages 35 and 36.

Open with shown above lets you choose from several apps to open a particular file. For example, a photo can be opened in **Paint**, **Photos** and **Windows Photo Viewer**, etc.

Folders can be copied, moved, deleted, renamed, etc., in a similar way to *files*, as just described.

OneDrive Cloud Storage

Windows 10 includes the OneDrive app and 5GB of free storage in the "clouds", i.e. large Internet computers. OneDrive is Microsoft's cloud storage system and other systems include Dropbox, Google Drive and iCloud. Your files in OneDrive are stored on the Web and in a folder in the internal storage on your device in your **Users** folder.

The OneDrive Web storage is listed in the left-hand panel of the File Explorer, as shown on the right.

There is also a local OneDrive folder on your internal storage. In the example below, the *local* **OneDrive** folder is on the hard disc drive **OS (C:)**, in the subfolder **Jim**, within the **Users** folder.

Files stored in OneDrive are accessible to you on *any* computer, tablet or smartphone connected to the Internet and with the OneDrive app installed. (As mentioned above OneDrive is already installed in Windows 10 but can also be installed on other platforms.)

Files saved in a common file format, such as **.pdf**, **.jpg**, etc., can even be opened on different platforms such as PCs, iPads, iPhones and Android tablets and smartphones.

Saving Files to OneDrive

In an app such as Word, Publisher or Excel, etc., select **File** and **Save As** then select **OneDrive** as the save location.

Alternatively you can copy or move files to OneDrive using **Copy** or **Cut** and **Paste** or drag and drop in the File Explorer as discussed earlier.

Automatically Saving Photos to OneDrive

Photos you take with a built-in camera or import from an SD card or flash drive are automatically saved on your device in the **Pictures** folder in **This PC**. In the **File Explorer**, under **This PC**, right-click or hold and release **Pictures**, then select **Properties**. Select **Location** and **Move** then **OneDrive** and **Pictures** then **OK**. All photos you take with your device or import from SD cards or flash drives, etc., will now go straight to your OneDrive folder.

Backing Up Important Files

When you add, edit or delete files in OneDrive on any device, all the changes are automatically *synced* to all your other devices. So files deleted on one device will also be removed from all the others.

Important files such as photos of special occasions, etc., should always be *backed up* to removable storage media such as flash drives, CDs, etc., by copying and pasting or dragging and dropping as discussed earlier.

Maintaining Your System

Deleting Unwanted Apps

You may wish to remove apps you no longer use, in order to save space on your internal storage such as a hard disc or an SSD (Solid State Drive). Click or tap the Start button in the bottom left-hand corner of the screen and click or tap the **All apps** icon shown on the right.

Scroll the **All apps** menu to display the app you wish to remove then right click or hold and release the name or icon for the app. Then select **Uninstall** from the pop-up menu shown on the right.

Alternatively, select **Settings** shown above, then click or tap the **System** icon shown on the right. Now select **Apps & features** and, if necessary, scroll to find the app you wish to remove. Click or tap the name of the app and then select the **Uninstall** button, as shown below.

System
Display, notifications, apps, power

Kindle
AMZN Mobile LLC

61.9 KB
19/11/2015

Move   Uninstall

Disk Clean-up

During the running of your computer, tablet or smartphone, *temporary files* are created and may accumulate, taking up valuable storage space. These can be safely deleted using Disk Clean-up. Select the **All apps** menu as described on the previous page and scroll down and select **Windows Administrative Tools** as shown below, then select **Disk Clean-up**.

After selecting the disc drive to be cleaned up you are given a report on how much space can be freed up.

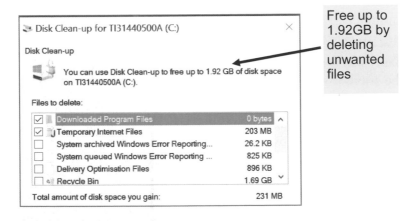

Free up to 1.92GB by deleting unwanted files

Tick any further files you wish to delete then select **OK** and **Delete Files** to free up the space on your internal storage.

Defragment and Optimise Drives

After a time, storage devices become fragmented after files are edited or deleted. This can cause a computer to slow down. *Defragmentation* reorganises the files to make the computer run efficiently. From the **All apps** menu scroll down to **Windows Administrative Tools** and select **Defragment and Optimise Drives** as shown on the previous page. The **Optimise Drives** window opens and you can select the **Optimise** button to carry out the optimisation immediately. There is also a **Change settings** button which allows you to schedule an automatic optimisation.

Status			
Drive	Media type	Last run	Current status
TI31440500A (C:)	Solid state drive	05/12/2015 19:27	OK (2 days since last run)

The Alternative Start Menu

This menu is opened after *right-clicking* or holding and releasing the Start button shown on the right.

The alternative Start menu contains many useful options, as shown in the small sample on the right.

The **Control Panel** has been the main settings tool in earlier versions of Windows and launches automatically in Windows 10 during certain tasks when using **Settings**. Or the **Control Panel** can be opened directly from the alternative Start Menu in Windows 10, as shown on the right.

Key Points: Managing Files and Folders

- A *file* is a document, image or app, etc., saved on backing storage such as a magnetic hard disc or solid state drive and given a *filename* by the user.

- A *filename* extension, such as **.docx**, is added to denote the type of file, as in **My CV.docx**. File types such as **.pdf** and **.jpg** are universally compatible.

- Files are managed in the *File Explorer* and organised in a series of *folders* created by the user.

- The **View** tab in the File Explorer allows files and folders to be displayed as icons of different sizes or listed with **Details** such as file types and sizes.

- Both files and folders can be managed after right-clicking or holding and releasing the file or folder in the File Explorer. Options include **Copy, Cut, Delete Send to** and **Rename**.

- Similar options are displayed on the *tabbed ribbon* across the top of the File Explorer window.

- OneDrive is an app built into Windows 10 and provides additional free storage on the Internet.

- Files in OneDrive are accessible to any computer with an Internet connection and a Microsoft account.

- Changes made on one computer, including deleting files, are automatically *synced* to the other machines.

- Photos taken with a built-in camera or imported from an external device can be saved directly to OneDrive.

- File maintenance includes deleting unwanted files, *defragmentation* and *backing up* important files to a storage medium such as a flash drive or CD.

Index